Contemporary
Islamic
Awakening

Studies in Islamic Thought (2)

Mohsen Araki

Contemporary Islamic Awakening

Phases and Pioneers

Translated by
Ali Soudani

Edited by
Najim al-Khafaji

Studies in Islamic Thought (2):

Contemporary Islamic Awakening
Phases and Pioneers

By : **Mohsen Araki**

First Published in Great Britain, 2001

Translated by: **Ali Abdallah Soudani**

Edited by: **Najim al-Khafaji, BA, MIL**

Published by:

BookExtra
INTERNATIONAL PUBLISHERS & DISTRIBUTORS

P.O.Box 12519,
London, W9 1ZA, UK
Tel: (44) 20 7604 5523
Fax:(44) 20 7604 4921
E-mail: sales@bookextra.com
Web site: www.bookextra.com

ISBN: **1 900560 28 3**

In The Name of God, The Beneficent, The Merciful

CONTENTS

FOREWORD

.After a prolonged period of stagnation and retreat, experienced by the Islamic *umma* (community) for many centuries past, alongside the dangers that were threatening its future and hindering its path and movement, Islamic awareness managed to surge forward in correcting these paths and finally achieving the hope Islamic nations were aspiring for in their search for salvation and self-assertion. This has come to the fore in the midst of a throng of conflicting theories and numerous challenges. And at last it had achieved what it had hoped for.

Our Islamic world had witnessed a number of changes from which it had emerged to fight, with firmness and clarity of purpose, for its existence. Just as a living being that grows and develops, Islamic awareness and the awakening of this nation together with its current renaissance were undergoing a process of integration as well, and still is, in firm strides and long leaps. This is being dealt with, by his eminence Ayatollah Mohsen Araki, in his book entitled, "Contemporary Islamic Awakening - Phases and Pioneers". The book discusses the features of this strategic change; whence this nation had marched forward, lead by its pioneers and renascent schools of thought, to finally achieve the dream of the prophets in establishing an Islamic state, right in the midst of all these challenges and adverse conditions.

The author has outlined three basic stages for the ongoing awakening the Islamic world is witnessing. He began with the efforts of Sayyid Jamaluddin Al-Asadabadi, well known as Al-Afghani, and his school of thought, in shedding lights on the dim situation and stirring the stagnation that then prevailed, and called this as the stage of "The Awakening".

At a time when the nation was in dire need for someone who could build and establish the intellectual basis and define its course and way of thinking, which emanates from an Islamic originality and apostolical principles, the author discusses this in a second stage that he named, "The Intellectual Build-up of the Nation". For this phase, the author has chosen Martyr Sayyid Mohammed Baqir as-Sadr, may his soul rest in peace, and paid tribute to other constructive contributions by other Islamic scholars in many a part of the Islamic countries. Then follows the third stage, of the Revolution and Establishment of the State, aimed at bringing up the Islamic *umma* to the level of initiative-taking in all those confrontations. For this stage, the author has chosen Imam Sayyid Rohullah al-Mosawi al-Khomeini, may Allah be pleased with him, as the founder of the Islamic state in modern times.

In the last two phases, the author sets forth detailed accounts of these two great pioneers. This is mainly due to the fact that he was a contemporary, a close associate and a student of theirs. No doubt, this study contains a number of attestations and details that could rarely come together in one comprehensive study.

BookExtra would like to take this opportunity in presenting this distinguished and new study of the modern cultural renaissance in our Islamic world, in the hope that a defined picture of this Islamic awakening has been made available through this study, which can be called a field study. What distinguishes this study is that it is presented by one of the contemporary intellectuals, the author of this book, who has lived in close proximity and in the heart of those transformations, especially the last two stages.

Dr. H. Bashir
Managing Director
BookExtra Ltd.

INTRODUCTION

One of the things that are most painful to a group of people, and I am one of them, is to review the history annals of nations that have gone into deep slumber, numbed by auxiliary past verbs, such as "I was", "Our fathers were" and "We have had glories". It suffices to say that they are auxiliary, i.e. incomplete past verbs. It is belittling that one is proud of what is incomplete regarding (actions).

It is even more bitter and hurtful to the soul when one reads the annals of history of bygone men, especially if they were succeeded by incompetent ones, as is the case of most of us today. It goes without saying that we almost have nothing to be proud of except reminisces of the past. It seems as though we have sufficed ourselves to be sitting on the fence, repeating with the old poet Amr bin Kulthoom:

If a suckling of ours reaches weaning time,
Tyrants would kneel for him prostrating!

As if those tyrants have no business other than waiting for the weaning period of one of our sucklings, only to kneel for him in prostration. Or, as if our newly-born came from a race other than the human race. It looks as though we are apt to believe in this fabrication and more of the like of it, lulled into pleasant dreams, that are not like the dreams of Joseph's inmates in his prison cell, or like the dreams of living nations that aspire for justice, security and peace, such who make the necessary effort to turn their dreams into reality that is experienced by living people. Alas, our dreams are but day dreams that have become one of the constant necessities of a life   that we think is a living, or a tranquil living that we live under its shades, repeating with the disappointed poet his saying:

> *Wishes if they had been, would have been the best of wishes,*
> *Otherwise, we would have lived with them a pleasant time!*

Yet, we do not do much worth mentioning in order to make true such wishes, as though dreaming of making them real should suffice!

In the differences, contradictions and exaggerations that riddle the history of our Islamic *Umma,* some people have discovered a praise for their own egos and symbols on the one hand, and a vilification of others and their symbols; this is more true in the histories of religious sects, thoughts and biographies; they try to find an excuse to drive them away from them, without trying to find an alternative to what already exists, rather than what ought to exist

In such an atmosphere clouded over with falsity, laziness and mistrust, those bent on vagaries have relished the task of trumpeting others' calls and slogans, of "contemporaneous" and "modernity", and what preceded and followed them, or what shall come after those. Those senseless people do all this without sufficient understanding of the meanings of such terms, or what they entail of painstaking work and diligence based on living principles that lie deep in the heart of the *umma* itself. This is mainly the reason for the appearance of a number of denominations, ideologies, organisations and parties that did not offer to our societies much more than backwardness that is marked with brutality and violence, a matter that added further to the splintering of people and implanted disunity and strife amongst individuals of the one society and one country. This damaging and devastating trend only met success because we have accepted psychological defeat in our "contest" with slogans and bright lights that won the minds of the benumbed who found it pleasing to slumber on the side walks of history whilst the others march firmly and move from one discovery to another invention, and from control of world riches to control of the people's feelings, senses and even hopes and dreams.

To be truthful, just like others, I am often swept with embittered feelings when resorting to the painstaking task of reviewing biographies of men and histories of nations that have resigned themselves to disappointments and abandonment; and generally speaking, those are exchanging accusations of defamation, infidelity and debauchery. Each of the two protagonists could either be unjust or just; one is on this side and the other on the other side; and it is obvious that they are not well versed in the language of dialogue, nor do they understand the reality they live in. That is why I keep at a distance, away from such books and volumes of reference. Should an urgent matter force me to look for the whereabouts of a certain place, or references that deal with a certain period of history, I find myself struggling with feelings and emotions, hardly able to bring patience back, and realising at the same time that hardships of scrutiny are unavoidable tasks imposed upon the researcher. One of these impositions is that you should possess sufficient awareness that enables you to differentiate between black and white, from amongst the heaps left over by certain circumstances that were camouflaged, sometimes, with blind prejudice that many regimes found fit to inflame further. To the mute texts of geography and history, I often retort the poem:

> *You are like the night that descends upon me,*
> *Though ample I imagined was the distance.*

But, is that a quality attributable only to all peoples of our nation and its men, at all times?!

The answer to this question is in a study entitled, "Contemporary Islamic Awakening - Phases and Pioneers", written by Ayatollah Mohsen Araki. The author intended it to be one of the studies that deal with certain aspects of Islamic awakening, revealing the existence of a thread that joins between Jamaluddin al-Asadabadi al-Afghani, Mohammed Baqir as-Sadr and Imam Khomeini.

The study takes the reader on a journey of reminiscing to the streets of Asadabad, al-Kadhimiya and Khomein, the towns and cities where the three pioneers were born. The author did not take the reader to the thoroughfares, localities and mosques of those cities, rather he took them to three of their men, that were equipped, through their suffering and struggle with backwardness in all its manifestations for which they were sent to prison on one occasion and exile in another, to enter history from its widest doors. In dealing with this, it is as though the author is repeating what a poet had said:

> *Abodes I pass, Layla's abodes,*
> *Anointing this and that wall*
> *Not the love of abodes that captivated*
> *my heart,*
> *But the love of those who*
> *dwelt in them!*

He was not concerned with narratives about walls. Rather he was concerned with delving into the lives of those whom Sheikh Araki describes as the ones qualified to enter history; the ones that dwelt in those (abodes), because he saw them and they have had their names recorded in the register of mortality. In the hearts of people, there was yearning for them, as well as homage and inspiration for a pristine struggle (*jihad*). The author attributes this to a common goal of the three pioneers who contributed to the nation's rise from its slumber and towards ridding it of the cloak of barren civilisation and intellectual inertia, since this rising is the most assured means to catch up with fast marching times towards the morrow. History does not stop, and it does not turn to those sleeping on its faraway and distant margins.

From here, Sheikh Araki began the subject of his study, with no need for an introduction, no hesitation at meanings of words or conflicting opinions of establishing this or that of tales of history. On the contrary, his first sentence set to define the path, and to where the author desires his reader to arrive at. In his study, the author discusses three men whom he considers the fathers of contemporary Islamic awakening. In this manner he starts his dialogue with the reality, forging ahead not from stylistic generalities that could have pushed me forcibly to the undesired task of searching into the mute pages of old history books, that I struggle with myself using all my inner force that those books would open for me a window to see through when a certain study or dialogue requires me to return to them.

Hence, the surprise that awaits the reader; the study focuses on three pioneers, to whom the author wholly devotes his study; he considers them to have mapped, for the nation, a course of progress and liberation from slavery, servitude and the regime's terrorism, that is overt sometimes and implicit most of the time.

Sheikh Araki looks into the text of his subject defining its time and place; his aim was not to sidewalk the walls that

surround that time and place. The author looks into the
multifaceted revivalistic efforts, such as those that appeared in
Syria in the North, Yemen and Oman in the South, Pakistan in
the East and Lybia and Algeria in the West; it is imperative,
however, not to overlook revivalistic and reformist movements
in Sudan, Nigeria and the Niger river basin – but here is not the
proper place to discuss these. Sheikh Araki divides the stages of
contemporary Islamic awakening into three, namely:

◊   The birth stage, which the author considers as its
    godfather the great spiritual reformist Sayyid Jamaluddin
    al-Asadabadi, well known as al-Afghani.

◊   The stage of the intellectual build-up of the nation,
    which the author considers the Martyr Imam Sayyid
    Mohammed Baqir as-Sadr as its outstanding representative.

◊   The stage of revolution and establishment of the state,
    whose great pioneer and supreme leader was Imam Sayyid
    Rohulla al-Khomeini. The thread that joins these stages is
    what we can call the "Will of Revival".

The author realises that confining the discourse to those
three pioneers lacks both objectivity and preciseness, since
those pioneers did not come from a void, nor did blessed winds
carry them over from faraway places, nor had they little in
common with peoples' sufferings and concerns, nor did they
descend from another planet. Our author realises this fact, and
ascertains that they are the sons of Islam with all its heritage
and presence, who not only studied under the supervision of
other outstanding jurists, but had surpassed texts of books to
reality, and rid themselves of fragility common with their likes
to the vigour they were well known for. As a consequence, the
first two went to meet martyrdom; whilst the third of those

managed to bring the ship, so to speak, to the shores of safety and security, by laying the foundations for the first Islamic republic in all history - according to what the author has reiterated at more than one occasion during his narrative.

In this active perspective that looks always ahead, the author goes to mention the names of many in whom he had found readiness for sacrifice and a wealth of achievements, and went to focus on their roles during the dangerous events that our Islamic world had witnessed. Examples of these are the "Tinbak - tobacco - Revolution" in Iran at the beginning of the last century, the "Revolution of 1920" in Iraq, the "Nationalisation Revolution" in Iran, and the religious reform movements in Iraq. The author did not deviate beyond the scope of these, neither in place nor in time, so as to remain within the field of his study that aims at discovering the ever growing and developing line that bound the efforts of those three pioneers.

On the other hand, and on the edges of time and place chosen by Sheikh Araki, there were growing and sizeable intellectual changes that came to bear fruit of a new reality that differed from one place to another, namely:

From Aleppo in Syria, came the thoughts of Abdul Rahman al-Kawakibi, who was an embodiment of Jamaluddin al-Afghani in many respects, including embarking on extensive travels and residing in Egypt. This had offered both men with the opportunity to have followers, students and disciples. Both were at odds with the Egyptian government of the time.

Maybe the only difference was that Jamaluddin had traveled to both oriental as well as Western cities; he was born in Asadabad; he visited Iraq, Egypt, India, Mecca and Istanbul, in addition to travels made to Europe. As for al-Kawakibi, his travels were mainly in the East. He visited Egypt, Yemen, Oman, Basra, Mecca and Medina, as well as other cities. In all these travels, he was looking here, investigating there and, in all, inflaming the spirit of revival.

In 1930, Mohammed Iqbal criticised, in broad terms, both Eastern and Western practices, calling for an independent Islamic revival that is free from exploitation and not hijacked by empty slogans. Iqbal saw that humanity was in need of three matters: a spiritual explanation for the universe, a spiritual liberation of the individual, and universal basic principles that direct the human society's development on a spiritual level. He concluded that Europe's idealism never came to be a vital factor in its life; he went further to conclude that it (Europe) had created a corrupt nature that search for its narrow-sighted interests through democracies – as Iqbal saw - that are sensitive to these interests whose prime function is the exploitation of the poor for the good of the rich. It is what Imam Khomeini had also called at the time, and reiterated later, as the exploitation of the meek by the tyrants.

Further afield, there appeared Omar al-Mukhtar in Lybia, and Abdul Hameed bin Badis in Algeria. The former led an armed uprising, whilst the latter organised the Islamic Scholars Revival Society. It is evident that the word "revival" in the name of the society had a significant meaning in this context, a matter that would later be developed further by the Algerian intellectual "Malik bin Nabi". It is well known that the evident goals of both al-Mukhtar and bin Badis were to spread awareness and to create the "Will for Revival" in order to get rid of the Italian and French colonialists from Lybia and Algeria, and to build the country anew on the basis of Islam. These in themselves were the first fruits of the calls voiced by

Jamaluddin al-Asadabadi, clearly manifested in the ideas of the Algerian intellectual Malik bin Nabi.

In the South of the Arabian peninsula, there appeared Sheikh Abdullah ibn Hameed al-Salimi and other religious scholars (*ulema*) of Oman, who worked strenuously in restoring awareness of the nation's history past and present. This added to the rapid attempts in revitalising reformist and reawakening ideas inherent in the Omani heritage, until those ideas were allowed to materialise in the restructuring of the state that was inaugurated in 1970 and the adoption of rebuilding the present upon the basis of the lively heritage and civilised history of Islam. In this, the idea of independent juridical judgement (*ijtihad fiqhi*) was adopted, as a part of the general jurisprudence in all aspects of life, in addition to the adoption of people's participation in running their affairs by themselves on the basis of the principle of consultation (*shura*).

This was the first official adoption of religious jurisprudence in the Arab world. Prior to this, talk about such jurisprudence was confined to the circles of religious jurists and scholars (*ulema*). It is hard to find an Arabic official text that discusses this subject, with the exception of the official Omani address which not only called for the rehabilitation of religious jurisprudence but also the legal incorporation and actual justifications for such incorporation, based on the fact that Allah, the Most High, has sent down the Qur'an with the wisdom and proclamation, and He has included in it the general principles and overall rules of religious precepts, but did not mention partial matters that change with time and place. This has been so as to avail Muslims of the chance to practise independent juridical judgement (*ijtihad*) in religious knowledge and understanding and to deduce interpretations that could suit new occurrences pursuant to their own environment and time.

Yet, in arriving at such rulings, they should apply strict adherence to the general principles and overall rules.

When Islam spread, following the Prophet's era, new matters surfaced when Muslims required the opinion of religious jurisprudence to sort them out. What did they do? They resorted to independent juridical judgement (*ijtihad*) and went on to derive the appropriate precepts. Then the official Omani address goes on to discuss Muslims' backwardness and its consequences. It concluded that the inertia that Muslims had resigned themselves to is incompatible with the nature of Islam; the address thus took this as a launch-pad to call for doors to be opened once again for practising independent juridical judgement; it also called for rewriting history on the basis of Logical Principles of Induction, for conclusions to be drawn out of its events.

In Pakistan, there appeared the ideas of Abul A'ala al-Mawdudi, in whose ideas and those of Jamaluddin al-Afghani's many researchers find a connection. That is, in the same way the ideas of Sayyid Jamaluddin's thought had found its way to a number of students who were prominent amongst their people, such as Sheikh Mohammed Abda and his disciple Mohammed Rasheed Redha. Al-Mawdudi took his ideas from the disciples of Sayyid Jamaluddin in Egypt.

If Mohammed Rasheed Redha was met with failure because he had attempted to unite two grossly opposing ideas, we find Abul A'ala al-Mawdudi having success in formulating a course particular to him, that was later taken up in Egypt, where it had clear effects, by Sayyid Qutub and others.

We have described his (al-Mawdudi's) course as particular to him, since the espousal of violence is not based on an exact understanding of Qur'anic stipulations. Violence has its own specific reference and place, and by no means has it a prevailing course in Islamic thought; in addition, violence is forbidden in Islamic *shari'a* law, if it sanctions murder of innocents or infringes upon the rights of other Muslims whom no one has the right to declare as unbelievers or warrant their bloodletting. We cannot call a movement that permits murder, terror and, with no right, declares other Muslims as unbelievers, a reform movement, let alone genuinely Islamic.

Based on this, we can say that Abul A'ala al-Mawdudi's course, insofar as its aspect of declaring some believers infidel (*takfeer*) is concerned, is peculiar to his own way of thinking, and did not have any impact on the figures discussed in Sheikh Araki's study. As far as Jamaluddin al-Asadabadi is concerned, he appeared long before al-Mawdudi declared his thoughts. The other two pioneers, Sayyid as-Sadr and Imam Khomeini, never were proponents of violence. On the contrary, they acted in accordance with the constraints of the tolerant Islamic *shari'a* law that is agreed upon by the Muslim public, religious scholars, theologians and intellectuals.

If Abul A'ala al-Mawdudi in Pakistan, and Mohammed Rasheed Redha in Egypt, were bereft of the thought of Sayyid Jamaluddin, in his study, Sheikh Araki proves the existence of an undeniable and uninterrupted connecting line that runs between Jamaluddin al-Asadabadi, Sayyid as-Sadr and Imam Khomeini. This connecting line comprises two aspects:

1. The theoretical aspect, or the intellectual dimensions. During the awakening stage that is represented by Asadabadi, Sheikh Araki reiterates that Muslims inaugurated their first steps towards reform following the example of the Hussainite revolt's goal. "I have not

marched out exuberantly or wantonly, but seeking to reform the religion of my grandfather, the Apostle of God". During the stage of the intellectual formation of the *umma*, the intellectual dimensions grew, flourished and were culminated through the unparalleled genius of Sayyid as-Sadr, as the author saw, not forgetting the efforts of other theologians. However, the author sufficed himself with concentrating on the role of as-Sadr, probably because he may have concluded that he was the most prominent amongst his peers and adversaries, and the most genius, intelligent and sacrificial.

After the two stages, the awakening and intellectual formation of the *umma*, comes the third phase which Sheikh Araki describes as the stage where the transfer of ideas into practical application was accomplished successfully by Imam Khomeini, may his soul rest in peace, through the establishment of the Islamic state and the foundation of its institutions, and offering the people an opportunity to develop itself, construct its own country for the present and future generations, according to Sheikh Araki's reading of events.

2.   The practical aspect, which is not limited to the dissertations put forward by each one of these pioneers, but to actual accomplishments on the ground. What Skeikh Araki puts forward indicates to us a fact worthy of attention. He remarks that the only one, amongst these three pioneers, who managed to translate ideas into reality was Imam Khomeini. Sayyid al-Afghani's, and Sayyid as-Sadr's dissertations remained within the theocratical sphere – especially those that dealt with the establishment of the state, not denying that Sayyid as-

Sadr, may his soul rest in peace, had succeeded on the practical level by participating in the foundation of the Islamic organization in Iraq. The said organisation actually started well before the time of Sayyid as-Sadr, a matter that manifested itself partly in the establishment of the "Islamic Revival Party" by Sheikh Mohammed Jawad al-Ha'eri during the revolution of 1920 in Iraq, but ceased activity for a time till it surfaced again in the mid-fifties of the last century; since then, its fortunes turned from glory to withdrawal.

As for his other initiatives, such as the one that dealt with reforming the Shia Religious Authority, especially in the Holy City of Najaf (Iraq), seemed premature, and as we shall see later on, had no great impact upon the Najaf seat of religious learning and knowledge (*hawza*) till now. His efforts were similar to those of Jamaluddin al-Asadabadi who lived in Najaf for four years, and had his own opinions and views regarding those Islamic seminaries and the way to develop their functions. Where the two differed is that Sayyid as-Sadr had surpassed the dissertations of Sayyid Jamaluddin. This is because as-Sadr was in close living proximity to that *hawza*, or Shia religious authority, after leaving Kadhimiyya for Najaf (two of the holy cities in Iraq) and stayed in the latter till he won martyrdom. This stay in Najaf availed him of the chance to be closely acquainted with the burdens and problems of the (*hawza*), and to propose solutions for them.

Whereas Jamaluddin (al-Afghani) al-Asadabadi's most important relationship was limited, during his stay in Najaf, to his studentship with the reformist Sheikh Murtadha al-Ansari, a matter that al-Asadabadi must have been proud of – as he had begun his studies at the age of twelve. I have no doubt that those years were the kindling sparks that inflamed the revivalist constructive ideas of al-Asadabadi, not only within the field of the Shia Religious Authority, but also at the level of the Islamic world affairs and the urgency of extricating it from backwardness and degradation - then dominant - to enlightenment and progress.

Sheikh Araki reiterates that in spite of concentrating his efforts on situations in Iran, Imam Khomeini lectures that he was giving in his sessions in Najaf were communicated to people outside. Moreover, and during his stay there, he had written many valuable studies regarding the Islamic state which had resounding impact on intellectuals and religious scholars alike, and from whose ideas they went on to launch their struggle for that aim.

In reviewing each of the three stages of his study, the author has followed each of the pioneer's life circumstances, his project for transforming the Islamic landscape, and his outstanding achievements. Evaluating the contribution of each pioneer, the author defines his own stand point towards those achievements, which differed from one pioneer to the other, namely:

A. Jamaluddin al-Asadabadi, alias al-Afghani, whom the author sees his outstanding achievements as:

   • Spreading awareness amongst the peoples of the Islamic *umma*,
   • Transcending national and sectarian barriers, and
   • His continuous call for the elimination of colonialism and dependency.

The author also mentions the negative aspects that faced Sayyid Asadabadi, especially his numerous travels from one country to another, due to harassments and irksome tracking down, a matter that weakened his relationship with the people and shrouded him with a cloak of ambiguity and obscurity amongst the ranks of his contemporary Shia religious scholars – even after his departure.

B.   The author's evaluation of   Sayyid as-Sadr's prominent achievements is:

- His studies were   a vital factor that gave immunity to the intellectual mind in the Islamic ranks in their confrontation   with   the   onslaught   of   Western culture,
- Promoting   the   (Islamic)   organisational   effort, Sheikh Araki lists his own remarks regarding this effort in the light of circumstances that surrounded it, and
- Setting off of the Islamic revolution in Iraq, at a time when Sayyid as-Sadr had not yet ascended to the office of Supreme Religious Authority - which the *umma* considers as the authority that has the final say in religious decision-making, as the author describes it.

C.   Imam Khomeini's achievements, as the author saw, are embodied in:

- Revival of the Islamic *umma* (community).
- Preparing steadfast and believing popular bases.
- Putting an end to the myth of separating religion and state.

- Resurrecting the idea of Islamic unity.
- Overthrowing the Shah's regime.
- Establishing the Islamic system of government upon a constitution that emanates from The Qur'an and *Sunna* (Prophet's tradition), and founding a new Islamic civic society.

Sheikh Araki then goes on to outline his evaluation of these achievements, indicating that there were unavoidable pitfalls that had accompanied the procession. Yet, these obstacles can be overcome through the meeting of free goodwill, as this *umma* - unlike others – has offered humanity one of the most noble civilisations, and can do the same once again through unity and the abolition of backwardness in all its manifestations and phenomena.

Dr. Hadi Hassan Hammoudi

GLOSSARY

Here is a list of frequently used terms and words,
mainly of Arabic origin, alongside their English translations.

a.s.:	An acronym for *allaihis salaam* - May peace be with him/them (the Infallibles).
C.E.:	Common Era
Eid:	Festivity, marking the end of fasting the Holy month of Ramadhan, or the end of *Hajj.*
Faqih:	Jurist.
Fatwa:	*Religious edict or ruling.*
Fiqh:	Jurisprudence.
Hawza ilmiyya:	Religious school or Islamic seminary.
Hijab:	Muslim women code of dress
HL:	*Hijri* Lunar Calender (dating back to the immigration of the Prophet Mohammad (*s.a.w.*). from Mekkah to Medina).
HS:	*Hijri* Solar Calender (Iranian Calender).
Irfan:	Gnosis.
Ijtihad:	Lit. Exertion — the ability to exercise independent legal judgment, using the traditional juridical tools.

Jihad:	Work in Allah's cause.
Marji':	The erudite jurist who has attained the level of reaching independent legal judgment and eventually assumes the office, or title, of Religious Authority.
Marji'yya:	The office, or title, of Religious Authority.
Mujahideen:	Freedom fighters.
Mujtahid:	A religious scholar (jurist), who has reached the level of practicing independent legal judgment, through his study and probity, using the traditional juridical tools).
s.a.w:	An acronym for *sallal lahu alaihi wa'alih wasallam* - May peace be with him (the Prophet) and his Pure Progeny.
Shari'a:	Islamic Divine law.
Sunna:	Prophet's tradition, i.e. his actions and sayings.
Taghut:	Despots.
Ulema:	Religious scholars, or the Muslim clergy.
Umma:	Islamic - transnational - community.
Usoolil fiqh:	Principles of jurisprudence.
Walayatul faqih:	The concept of "The guardianship of the jurist, or jurist-ruler".

Preamble

All praise is due to Allah, Lord of the Worlds, and may His prayer and peace be with Mohammed and his pure descendants

Since its inception a century ago, the Islamic awakening went through three basic phases:

1. The Birth Stage, which can be called the wakefulness stage, when the *umma* had just begun to awake from its long slumber that lasted centuries on end, where it started to regain its life and rise up from its slumber. Sayyid Jamaluddin al-Husayni al-Asadabadi, known as al-Afghani, was the man of this stage and its pioneer.

2. The stage of intellectual development of the *umma* (Islamic community), and coinage of the Islamic theoretical thinking that enabled it to maintain its confrontation with the materialistic schools of thought, as embodied by Communism, Socialism and Capitalism, which presented it with the chance of rebuilding itself once again in the light of Islam's understandings and principles. This stage is considered most detrimental in the history of Islamic awakening. Its greatest pioneer and unparalleled leading figure Martyr Imam Mohammed Baqir al-Sadr.

3. The stage of revolution and establishment of the state, and the full identification of the *umma*, with the revolution, in the field, resumption of its life with all its basic fundamentals. This phase is also concerned with establishing the Islamic state on new structure that is compatible with developments of time and demands of the

present day.   The pioneer of this stage, and great leader, is the supreme Imam Sayyid Rohulla al-Mosawi al-Khomeini.

In this brief study, it is not possible to look into each of these three stages in detail; rather we shall, in this summation, attempt to shed some light on the role undertaken by each one of those great luminaries in the building of the current Islamic awakening in its three stages.

In our study, we shall deal with the achievements of each of these three leaders in a chronological order within the stage they led, and discuss each one in four chapters. Chapter one - brief account of the life of each of those leaders. Chapter two - a summary of the project for change espoused by each one of them. Chapter three - their achievements. Chapter four - an evaluation of their ideas and achievements.

Phase I

Awareness and Birth

of

Islamic Awakening

Awareness and Birth of
Islamic Awakening

The Islamic *umma* (community) was in a deep and prolonged coma. From East to West, ignorance and retardation dominated. Islamic countries were subject to the invasions of colonialists, plunder of marauders, their destinies, a matter outsiders manipulate as they desired, whilst Muslim rulers, religious leaders and men were unaware of all of that, or were in a state of weakness and impotence, or at best helpless and powerless, where all avenues to rise and march were closed. This was the state of the Islamic *umma* at the time Sayyid Jamaluddin (Al-Asadabadi) began his revivalist movement. He toured the Islamic countries east and west, bearing his call to the people to come alive, to act and rise. Thus, starting the first stage of Islamic awakening by arousing the *umma* from its slumber and rekindling elements of life and strength inherent in it. The pioneer of this stage was Sayyid Jamaluddin al-Asadabadi, well known as al-Afghani.

« Chapter one »

A Short Biography

Sayyid Jamaluddin was born in Sha'ban 1254 HL (1823 CE) in Asadabad of Hamadan Province[1] , a well known city in Iran. He died in Shawwal 1314 HL (1898 CE) in Istanbul[2].

Sayyid al-Amin al-Aamili reported in his work entitled A'ayaan ash-Shi'a - Shia Luminaries, "As for his being ascribed to Afghanistan and being known by the al-Afghani, this was one of the titles which has no basis – and many such titles are of no origin. The reason for being renowned by that name was that he had attributed himself to the Afghans, in Egypt and other countries he visited, and not to Iran, as a guise. Had it been otherwise, he would have not won the reputation of, "The wise man of Islam and philosopher of the East". Nor had he won this wide repute, nor would *al-Sadr al'adham* (supreme leader) of Istanbul had showered him with the honour that he befittingly deserved. al-Aamili goes on to mention, "Nor would Sheikh Mohammed Abda (of Egypt) have taken him for a companion, taken learning from him, and had him as mentor and close friend, etc." [3]

Al-Aamili quotes Sayyid Salih ash-Shahristani in *al-Irfan* Magazine as saying, "Sayyid Safdar, father of Sayyid Jamaluddin, came to Tehran with his son Jamaluddin in early with his son Jamaluddin in early 1266 HL (1849 CE). After they had stayed

---

(1) A'ayan ash-Shi'a : vol.4/p.206
(2) *Sayyid Jamaluddin va Andishehay-e ou* (Sayyid Jamaluddin and His Thoughts), p.490
(3) A'ayan ash-Shi'a : vol.4/p.207

there for more than five months, they travelled to Iraq and entered the city of Najaf at the time of Sheikh Murtadha al-Ansari.

Sheikh al-Ansari looked after Jamaluddin, and Sayyid Safdar remained, in Najaf, for two months before returning to Asadabad. The young Jamaluddin remained in Najaf for four years".[1]

In his book "The Present Islamic World", Luthrut Stomard said, "Jamaluddin was a master of the wise genius, prince of eloquent speakers, smartest of the artful, of a strong argument, keen proof, staunch, ardently determined, and of an intense stateliness; as if in his human nature were the secrets of magnetism. That is why the course he had followed was great, and his conduct unparalleled. That has placed him amongst Muslims in a position rarely attained by others. He travelled widely in each one of the Islamic countries; he also visited European countries one by one, and gained from these great travels deep knowledge and vast understanding of the nations' histories and the world. All that gave him deep-rooted knowledge, fathomed many a hidden secret and mysetery, which greatly assisted him in undertaking the outstanding tasks that he did."[2]

In his preface to Sayyid Jamaluddin's paper, which refutes the atheists (free thinkers) ideas, Sheikh Mohammad Abda wrote, "...and he (Sayyid Jamaluddin) had completed his studies at the age of eighteen, after which he was offered the chance to travel to India, where he stayed for a year and few months.

---

(1) A'ayan ash-Shi'a: vol.4/p.207
(2) The Present Islamic World, translated by Ajaj Nuwayhidh, vol.1 / p. 135.

There he availed himself of the study of mathematical sciences in accordance with the new European approach. As for his political aim to which he had directed his thinking, strived for all his life, and for the cause of which he withstood all that had befallen him, was the uplifting of the Islamic state from its weakness and making it aware of looking after its affairs, so that the *umma* would catch up with other mighty nations and the state with other powerful states, thus Islam would regain its status and the true religion its glory. In all this, he strived for the bringing down of Britain's influence in Eastern countries and diminishing its (long cast) overshadow upon the *umma*. Accounts of his enmity to the English, that are lengthy to describe in detail, abound.

He went on to say, "He never contended with anyone unless he prevailed, nor entered into an argument with a scholar without compelling him to surrender; the Europeans conceded this to him after the Easterners acknowledged the same. On the whole, if I was to describe what Allah has bestowed upon him, of a sharp intellect, capacity of mind and great insight, then I would not be exaggerating to say that it was the utmost that has been bestowed upon other people, save the prophets. This is surely a grace of Allah that is bestowed upon whom He pleases, and Allah is of great grace".

Sheikh Mohammed Abda went on to mention, "He travelled to India at the age of 18, i.e. 1272 HL (1855-6 CE), where he stayed for a year and few months, after which he went to Hijaz (the coastline on the Red Sea embracing the Arabian Peninsula) for *Hajj* (pilgrimage); those travels lasted for nearly a year during which he moved from one country to another and from one province to another until he arrived at Mecca in the year 1273 HL (1856-7 CE). Through all these travels he had acquainted himself with many a custom of various nations he visited, fathomed their moral codes and gained many a benefit. After performing *Hajj*, he returned to his homeland. In the year 1285 HL (1868-9 CE), he went to *Hajj* via India. When arriving there, the Indian government received him with ceremony and honour, but did not allow him a longer stay in the country, nor did it permit religious scholars (*ulema*) to confer with him without the meddling of its men; thus, he could not stay there for more than a month. The government of India put him on one of its ships – at its own expense-heading to Suez (Egypt) where he arrived and stayed for about forty days, during which he often visited al-Azhar mosque. Then, he hurried to go to Astana (Istanbul); after a few days from his arrival there, he managed to meet *Al-Sadr Al-a'dham*, the Supreme Ruler, – Aali Pasha, who honoured him, accorded him the respect that was due to him and went to attend to him like he had not done to others before. Sheikh Abda then refers to a plot that was hatched against him (Jamaluddin) in Istanbul, and mentions, "He was ordered by *Al-Sadr Al-a'dham* to leave Istanbul for a few months.

He left Istanbul, knowing that he was unjustly treated ...and some of his associates advised him to turn to Egypt, which he had arrived at first Muharram 1288 HL; then Sheikh Abda goes on to say – his status was growing and people's hearts were yearning to meet with him, until Egypt's rule turned to the Khideiwi Tawfiq Pasha. Sayyid Jamaluddin was one of the supporters of the Khideiwi's aspirations and the proponents of his merits. But some of the evil doers, like the British Consul General – Mr. Vivien [sic], were ardently seeking to change the Khideiwi's heart against him, until the latter issued his orders that Sayyid Jamaluddin, and his servant Abu Turab should leave the country. He departed from Egypt to India in 1296 HL (1879 CE)., and resided in Hyderabad Addikin, in which he wrote his paper Refutation of the Freethinkers' Doctrine - *Nafie*

Mathhab Addahriyyin. After the last unrest in Egypt, Sayyid Jamaluddin was called from Hyderabad to Calcutta by the government of India which obliged him to reside in there until the disturbances in Egypt ceased. Then the English war started, and he was permitted to leave to any country he chose. He went to Europe. London was the first stop, where he stayed for a few days; he then moved on to Paris in which he remained for three years – during which we had met with him.

When he was commissioned by the Society of *Al-Urwatul Wuthqa*, literally, the firmest handle, in reference to verse 256/Chapter 2 of the Holy Qur'an", to set up a newspaper that call upon Muslims to unite under the banner of the Islamic Caliphate (May Allah supports it). He had asked me to supervise its edition and I accepted the offer. Eight editions of the paper were published; it had won the hearts of people in the East in general, and Muslims in particular, by a measure unrivalled by a vocal of preaching, nor an arousal of a warner, before. Obstacles arose that prevented the continuation of publishing the paper, as the doors of India were closed in its face, and the English government harassing those who received it. After this, Sayyid Jamaluddin stayed in Europe, a few months in Paris and others in London, until he had returned to Iran in early Jamadil Ula 1303 HL (1885-6 CE).

"In Iran, Sayyid Jamaluddin never resigned. He had started to spread awareness amongst the people, and explain to them the bitter reality of what had befallen them from weakness, humiliation and backwardness as a result of corrupt rulers, people's submission, the ignorance that prevailed over them and their low morale. One of his companions, Almirza Sadiq Khan al-Broujardi, had said of him – according to what Sayyid Salih ash-Shahristani, quoting al-Broujardi in *al-Irfan* Magazine – in all the gatherings he attended and the discussions he took

part in, he was criticising Sultan Nasiruddin, whose close
confidant then was Mirza Ali Asghar Khan, known as *Aminus
sultan* - Secretary of the Sultan, calling for reforms and resisting
tyranny. This led to his eviction from Iran to Iraq by order of
the minister of the Shah Nasiruddin. Sayyid Jamaluddin
described the state in which he was evicted to Iraq in his known
letter to Imam Shirazi in which he said, "...then I was forcibly
taken by his villains, while I was unwell of health, on a working
horse, chained, in winter snow falls and bitter winds. I was led
by a company of cavaliers to Khanaqin (near the border inside
Iraq) from which I was taken by a group of policemen to
Baghdad; I had written to the *Wali* (Governor of Baghdad),
pleading with him to send me to Basra, knowing that had I
been left to my affair, I would have come to your eminence and
relate his (the Shah's minister's) affairs and the state of the
umma (community), and to explain to you the evils that had
beset the lands of Islam. And I would have implored your
authority to come to the aid of the religion, and pleaded for the
aid of Muslims; he (the minister) was sure that had I the chance
to meet your eminence, he would not be able to remain in his
ministership that is built upon destruction of country and ruin
of people".

From Basrah, Sayyid Jamaluddin headed to Europe once
again. He stayed in London, and began to publish *Dhia'ul
Khafiqeen* Newspaper. This led to his harassment by the British
government, after which he was called by Sultan Abdul
Hameed to come to Istanbul. He went there in 1310 HL
(1892-3 CE). where he continued his activities which were
aimed at establishing one Islamic state and uniting the Islamic
umma (community); until the murder of Nasiruddin Shah in
1313 HL (1895-6 CE), by Aqa Riza Khan Kirmani who was a
close student of Sayyid Jamaluddin. The Iranian government
requested the Ottoman Court to hand over Sayyid Jamaluddin

after it had revealed to the Ottoman authorities the identity of Sayyid Jamaluddin and that he was an Iranian Shia. This led – as the researcher Murtadha Muddarisi Chahardhi saw – the Iranian government to conspire in order to assassinate him. It had sent a man called Nasirul-mulk who managed, with the help of the Iranian Embassy in Istanbul, to poison Sayyid Jamaludin; thus, he was murdered by poisoning and his martyrdom was in 1314 HL (1896-7 CE).

« *Chapter Two* »

His Project for Introducing Change

Sayyid Jamaluddin based his project for transformation on three pillars:

1. Spreading awareness amongst Muslim rulers, religious scholars and the masses, drawing their attention to the corruption and acute backwardness that dominated their cultural, social and political life, and calling them to work strenuously towards reforming that corrupt reality, with a view to renewing the religious presence in Muslims' life pursuant to the goals of the Mohammedan message, its principles and values.

Sayyid Jamaluddin wrote an article published in *Misr* - Egypt - Newspaper on 14 February 1879, which was republished by Rasheed Redha in *Almanar*'s issues of 4 and 14 November 1900, in which he said, "People of the East have long stayed under the yoke of tyranny of absolutists, whose differing whims emanate from contradiction of their nature and ill-breed, along with the absence of a deterrent that could deter them, an inhibitor that could inhibit them, and an outside force that could confront their march. This has led the tyrants to encroach upon their subjects and deny them their rights; they even necessitate manipulation of their instincts and moral codes, changing their human nature in the process, so much so that they became unable to distinguish between what is good and what is bad, the harmful and the useful; thus, they were on the verge of not knowing themselves, and what they embody of sacred forces and overall capacity, and absolute authority on the world of nature and the power of intellect to which all creations, simple and complex, submit and all fauna and flora obey its orders. Their prolonged lapse of indulging in superstitions that dulls the insight and necessitates total omission and lengthy bewilderment; even more than that, but it calls for reducing them to the order of animals, and their persistence for successive periods of time in contradicting real science, which unveils the truth about man, teaches him his duties and what he requires for living, explains to him the causes that lead to disorder of the social structure, which enables him to push them aside. It is an attempt to extinguish its light with foolish sayings they had inherited from their fathers and silly opinion and argument of diminishing wealth of its books and loss of their trace, to replace it with what they had made them fall into - the darkness that they shall never be guided to exit from". [1]

This is a sample of his utterances through which he was spreading awareness amongst Muslims, and enlightening them about the corrupt reality they live in, and call upon them to reform and change it.

2.   Abolition of colonial domination of Islamic countries, rekindling the spirit of independence and self-reliance in the Muslim nations, and even peoples of the East. All this was with a view to ridding them of the state of dependency and feeling inferior that had reigned over them and their leaders, and weakened their resolve against foreign hegemony. Their stand vis-a-vis foreign culture is that of a headless imitator.

---

(1) Unknown Works Series: Jamaluddin al-Afghani, p.62, Riad Arrayyis Publishers.

Sayyid Jamaluddin wrote in an article in *Al-Baseer,* which was published in Paris, issue dated 26 April 1883, "Nations have their ups and downs. In their rising or falling, they alternate between happiness and misery; they experience glory and wretchedness; as soon as they aspire for peeks of glory, they fall to a rock bottom misery once again... The reasons for nations' fall and ascension are not the same as those for a rise of a star or a setting of a planet, as some would like to explain. Neither low, nor high tide of its power is a result of natural causes, for we see many a nation that regained youth after old age, resurrected after being declared dead and its bones decayed; natural causes do not change norms or cease courses; alterations beset them not and variations of movements turn them not from their course. Here in front of your sight the Italian nation to prove the trueness of my divulgence; close your eyes not from Spain, considering the state it was in and what it has turned into. Rise of nations attained by their own deeds, their downfall also. For example, the Arab nation did not exceed two millions at the rise of Islam, and in spite of abject poverty then, absence of sciences and know-how, it had forced the Emperors of Persia into surrender and defeated the Caesars of the Romans; nowadays it numbers thirty million and unable to run its own affairs and impotent to safeguard their country. Ottomans, few in numbers, had made Western states tremble, and tyrants lowly..... for half a century – though vast their dominion and great their number – they appeal for mercy from kings of the *Ifrandj* (the Francs) and seek their protection, claiming life on earth is untenable without them. No nation can attain a measure of happiness without unity of its individuals in a manner akin to body organs; it shall not have the upper hand and extension of dominion until courses of its individuals are directed along the radii of a

circle that end up in one central point which represents the
happiness of all, unswerving outside the circumference of
nationality, and each should consider the interest of the
whole as well as himself, consider his own interest as well
as others so that riches of the whole would be like a spring
from which diverges rivulets of individuals' good". [1]

3.   Revival of Islamic *umma* (community) through full
application of Islamic rules, and uniting it under one
Islamic government.

   Sayyid Jamaluddin wrote in an article published by *Al-
Urwatul Wuthqa* (the Firmest Handle) under the headline,
"Muslims' Decline and Quiescence: The Causes":

"Muslims have a strong hold on religion, strength of faith
and firmness of conviction with which they rival other
nations... Despite this, we nowadays see some of the
followers of this religion oblivious to what befalls their
brethren and do not share their suffering. People of
Baluchistan watch (from close distance) movements of the
English [British] on the positions of their coreligionists, yet
remain unmoved, nor are they shocked at their brethren's
plight. Afghanis witness the English's interference in
Persia, with no sign of discomfiture or frustration on their
part ... Muslims cling to these tenets and the sense of the
just call inside them contradicts the state they are
witnessing, a matter that calls for surprise and causes
bewilderment; this, indeed, surpasses all explanations of
reason. Here is a summation for this: Ideas, religious faiths
and other psychic facts, concepts and sentiments, though
they are triggers of actions and from whose judgements

---

(1) Ibid, p.107

they are issued, by the Will of Allah, the All-mighty, the Knowing, yet the actions affirm and strengthen these, instill them in the psyche till they become what is called talent and disposition, upon which compatible influences accumulate... After pondering these explicit fundamentals, and perusing them with an eye of wisdom, the reason for Muslims quiescence to what they are in, despite their strong hold on religion, will be evident to you.

There remains little that binds Muslims except a religious faith devoid of actions....It was the duty of the *ulema*, honoured as inheritors of the prophets, to rise up in reviving religious bondage, and ironing out differences that occurred in relation to the ascension to power, so as to make possible reconciliation called for by religion; pursuant to this, they should take schools and mosques as venues for the continuous preaching of this reconciliation, till each school and mosque would become grounds for the revelation of the spirit of unity, and each would be a ring in one chain, should one of its ends be shaken the other end would shake in convulsions as a response". [1]

---

(1) *Al-Urwatul Wuthqa* p.30, 1ˢᵗ edition, Islamic Cultural Centre in Europe, Rome, Italy.

« Chapter Three »

Sayyid Jamaluddin's Achievements

Main Achievements

Sayyid Jamaluddin's achievements were many and great; here, we shall refer to the most outstanding among them:

A. Promoting awareness and revival in the Islamic *umma* (community), and propagating renascent Islamic ideas amongst the cadres, especially religious scholars and leading politicians. Sayyid Jamaluddin's efforts in this field were the beacons that guided various social changes in the Islamic countries.

Amongst these changes and transformations, which were brought about by Sayyid Jamaluddin's efforts, had been the events witnessed in India where Muslims took one united stand against British imperialism, and managed to safeguard their Islamic identity; their struggle culminated in the establishment of the Islamic state of Pakistan. Of the great transformations, which were precipitated by his ideas and efforts, was the Constitutional Revolution in Iran in 1324 HL (1906 CE). Although this revolution occurred after the lifetime of Sayyid Jamaluddin, yet examination of events, that preceded the constitutional revolution, were preludes to it. This would clearly indicate that the early shoots of political and ideological revival, which bore fruit in the eruption of the constitutional revolution, were the fruitions of the efforts of Sayyid Jamaluddin; he was first to implant the seeds of the transforming uprising in Iran towards the end of the Qajars' era. As for Egypt and North Africa, these were the most affected by the ideas of Sayyid al-Afghani or al-Asadabadi. The Islamic awareness movement in these areas, and the ideological and organisational activity that followed, were indebted as a whole, along with its preliminary foundations, to this great man. Dr. Mohammed al-Bahii said, "Jamaluddin died in 1897 after a violent struggle with Western colonial powers that lasted nearly thirty years; soon after his death, may Allah's mercy be with him, his struggle and thought had impacted eleven parts of the Islamic world, especially in those parts where foreign powers dominated and trifled with what Muslims hold sacrosanct, their dignity, economics and natural resources. Jamaluddin died, but his legacy lived to appear in Egypt through Mohammed Abda and his fundamentalist school of thought; in Algeria, in the form of Algeria Religious Scholars Society, founded by the late Abdul Hameed bin Badis (d.1940); in Indonesia, in the form of the Movement for the Renewal of *Almanar*, in India, in the Community of *Ahlul-Hadeeth*, and Religious Scholars' Forum, founded by Mohammed Shibl an-Nu'mani (d. 1941), and the Azhar of India in the School of Sciences House in Diobind that was transferred after the partition of 1948 to (Akori) in Peshawar, Pakistan". [1]

B.   Preparing a generation of religious scholars and activists of a revivalist Islamic thinking, who followed in the footsteps of Sayyid Jamaluddin in various Islamic countries of the Islamic world. The School of Jamaluddin has continued within these groups of thinkers and bearers of Islamic awareness till their effects appeared in many Islamic countries whether on the ideological or political levels.

---

(1) Modern Islamic Thinking and its relation to Western Imperialism, p.112

Dr. al-Bahii says, "Jamaluddin groomed a generation of leaders, that outlived him, possessing a foundation of

knowledge, a subtle and balanced enlightenment, on the basis of a correct understanding of Islam and its teachings, and in the light of a set of guidelines laid down by an experienced religious scholar.

Jamaluddin was not only a leader of a nation or nations fighting against a powerful and organised external enemy, but a pioneer of an idea and a sound understanding of Islam. Had it not been for Jamaluddin's Islamic scientific enlightenment, we would not have seen, after his departure, a personality like that of Sheikh Mohammed Abda, who is unique among his contemporaries in the understanding of Islam, discretion of its values and in the understanding of life and its circumstances. Nor would this comprehensive Islamic order for Islamic life under the teachings of Islam – like the one formulated by his faithful disciple Mohammed Abda – would have existed".

Evaluating Sayyid Jamaluddin's Achievements

An overall evaluation of Sayyid Jamaluddin's achievements can be summarised in the following points:

1. Sayyid Jamaluddin met with great success in promoting awareness in the Islamic *umma* (community) and in arousing its men, religious scholars and thinkers; he also succeeded in creating an effective current of active awareness and revivalist thinking amongst the intelligentsia in the Islamic society far and wide.

2. Sayyid Jamaluddin was distinguished from other leaders of Islamic awakening and its builders, in transcending national and ethnic divides, and in overcoming all obstacles that stand between interaction of all the *umma*'s sections. In spite of being an Iranian Shia, he managed to work with the Sunnite Turkish rulers and religious scholars, just as he did with the Iranians. He had worked with the clergy of al-Azhar Mosque of Egypt, just as he did amongst Shiite religious scholars in Iraq and Iran. This uniqueness of his character endowed him with influence upon men of the Islamic *umma*'s different sects and ethnic groups from East to West.

3. Sayyid Jamaluddin occupied an unrivalled position amongst Sunni religious scholars, so much so that they called him "Philosopher of the East" and the "Great Wise Man", adjectives indicative of his distinguished scientific and ideological position in the world of Sunni Islam, Yet, Sayyid Jamaluddin occupied neither a prominent scientific, nor an ideological position in the world of Shia Islam. Nor was he regarded by the elite of Shia religious seminary as a great thinker who had put forth new ideas in the world of thought and scientific research. In the Shia circles, Sayyid Jamaluddin was famed for being a reformist with new political ideas, calling for the liberation of Islamic countries and for reconciling differences and discord in order to stand up against colonial hegemony in one rank. That is why, in the countries where Sunni Muslims were in the majority, Sayyid Jamaluddin was lacking the social depth, for he was – in spite of his genius – an outsider. Yet, in the countries where Shia formed the majority, he was lacking the ideological and religious depth that might well have enabled him to occupy a leading role that could have qualified him to undertake what he was aspiring for, of

affecting an overall change in that traditional society, and turning it into a new Islamic society abound with justice and pulsating with life.

4. One of the reasons that left negative marks on the activity of Sayyid Jamaluddin and his revivalist movement the fact that he was always on the move, i.e. never staying in one particular place for long. In his arousing movement, this had denied him the opportunity to make the required impact on the societies he worked within. Nor was he able, through his drive for change, to acquire a network of relations in the social arena.

5. Because of all we have mentioned, and other reasons that are lengthy to detail, relation between Sayyid Jamaluddin and the Islamic general public, in the places that he used to frequent, was weakened. This weakness of relationship led to the light social weight he was enjoying, and consequently loss of sufficient protection and support that he could have relied on in executing his project for change. This was one of the important reasons that encouraged rulers and corrupt elements against him, in all the places he stayed in order to start this ideological and political activities. No sooner had he embarked on the first step of his project for transformation, the corrupt felt a danger on their interests and the positions they held, it was easy then to run him out, and they treated him with brutality and degradation, thus turning into a failure what he was aspiring for of building awareness amongst people and spreading his ideas and goals.

Phase II

Ideological Development

of

the *Umma*

Ideological Development of the *Umma*

It was imperative for the Islamic awakening to have, on the theoretical level, an Islamic ideology that sets out appropriate solutions for the problems of modern man, and present Islam as a comprehensive order that is in tune with time and harmony with the demands of the present epoch. A number of Islamic thinkers contributed to this field, but the theoretical output submitted by Martyr Imam as-Sadr was the most sound, comprehensive and deep, whether on the level of approach or essence.

Nearly half a century after what Sayyid as-Sadr has bequeathed, we still find it hard to place an Islamic thinker, who had so rich ideological output for solving the problems of contemporary man whether on the philosophical, economic or social levels, in the same league of the school of our master Sayyid as-Sadr, may his soul rest in peace.

Sayyid as-Sadr's thought has managed to fill a vast area of the ideological and theoretical void facing the Islamic awakening. Thus, we are justly entitled to consider the martyred Imam as-Sadr the one and only pioneer of the Islamic awakening on both the ideological and theoretical levels.

Here, we are unable to numerate the great impacts of the Sayyid's school of thought that are left on the ideological landscape of Islamic society as a whole, especially in the Shia dominion. Anyone following closely the development of the ideological landscape amongst Muslims towards the end of the twentieth century, can see the clear imprints of the new Islamic thinking, left by Imam as-Sadr, especially in the fields of philosophy, economics, religious jurisprudence (*fiqh*) and principles of jurisprudence (*usoolil fiqh*).

Hereunder is a short biography of this pioneering scholar and a resume of his achievements in the ideological development of the Islamic *umma*.

« Chapter One »

A Short Biography of Martyr Imam as-Sadr

Martyr as-Sadr was born in Kadhimiyya in Iraq on 25 Thil Qi'da 1353 HL (1934-5 CE).[1]

After finishing his primary schooling in Kadhimiyya, he moved to Najaf. During the years that he was attending his primary schooling, and in a personal effort of his, he was studying outside the normal school curriculum, attained advanced levels of learning, even before completing his primary schooling. After moving to Najaf, he continued his Islamic studies, which he had began in Kadhimiyya, on higher levels. He attended lectures in what is called "External Research"[2] soon after arriving in Najaf [3], while he was only twelve years of age and he gave up *taqleed* (lit. emulation - the following by a layman of a learned scholar 'jurist' in matters of religious practice) since he had reached the age of *takleef* (i.e. age of fifteen when it becomes incumbent on a male Muslim to uphold the precepts of religion) . This indicates that S ayyid

---

(1) The Martyr as-Sadr - Years of Affliction and Days of Siege, p.42.

(2) External Research is the highest level of Islamic studies in the Shiite Religious Seminaries (hawza), where theology students are being qualified for ijtihad (The ability to exercise independent legal judgement in religious matters, using juridical tools).

(3) Life of the Martyr as-Sadr, Introduction to the first seminar in al-Usool (Principles of Jurisprudence) p. 47, published by the Islamic Thought Academy.

as-Sadr had attained the level of *ijtihad* at such a tender age.[1]

Some great Najaf religious jurists pronounced him as having attained the level of *ijtihad* at the age of seventeen.[2]

He, then, continued his Islamic studies in the Holy Najaf University under the supervision of its renowned professors, until he completed his higher studies, to become an authoritative *mujtahid* (a religious scholar who has reached the level of practising independent juridical judgement, through his study and probity) in the year 1378 HL (1958-9 CE). He was highly acclaimed by his professors for his excellence and genius. He started lecturing and writing, which he had began, to some extent, before. He started writing at an early age; his first work included his own approach regarding the science of *usool* (principles of jurisprudence) in a book entitled " Purpose of Thought in the Principles of Jurisprudence ". This came with another scientific work in which as-Sadr looked into the events of Islamic history that immediately followed the death of the Messenger of Allah (*s.a.w.*) - May peace be with him and his pure descendants; it was published under the title, " Fadak in History ". He later started plans to publish a number of studies that dealt with outlining Islamic thought, as a faith and system, in a modern scientific style compatible with the then prevailing times and requirements. In it, he would bring Islam to the fore as an ideology, order and system, in a picture that reveals to the new world the compactness of the project designed by the Creator of heaven and earth for man. Sayyid as-Sadr has also shown the failure of temporal schools as well as materialistic

(1) Introduction to the Research in Science of *Usool*, vol. 1 of 2nd part /p.52, published in 1407 H.
(2) Ibid, p. 43

ideologies and theories that disengage (i.e. cut) man's relation with the revelation of heaven, bind him to earth's dust and close in his face the path ahead towards greatest happiness and sought after perfection. From here he started the first steps of his great work " Our Philosophy " in which he presents Islamic philosophical thinking in an unprecedented manner. His approach was that he discussed other philosophic trends, compared to Islam's philosophy, only to prove the power of Islam's logic and its sublime philosophy; in the process, he proved the failure of materialistic philosophy, weakness and impotence of their logic in combatting and standing up to Islamic thought in the field of philosophical research based on proof and tangible evidence.

Then he followed this with another piece of work " Our Economics ", in which he discussed modern economic schools of thought with scrutiny and investigation, made a comparison between what contemporary materialistic culture, both capitalist and socialist, has offered as (doctrinal) solutions for the tragedy of modern economic life, and that offered by Heaven's plan as embodied by the Islamic economic system. In this objective study, he highlighted major drawbacks and weak points inherent in the materialistic economic systems, both capitalist and socialist. He showed the superiority of Islam's economic doctrine over its rivals across the board, i.e. in basis, principles, precepts and details. In the introduction to " Our Economics ", he humbly described his intellectual effort thus, " This is but a preliminary attempt – regardless of its fortunes of success or elements of innovation - to fathom the economic thought in Islam and formulate it in an ideological cast upon whose basis would be built a towering edifice for Islamic economy, that is rich in philosophy and basic ideas, explicit in its general imprints, milestones and directions, defined in its relation, stand up to other major economic doctrines, yet forming an organic part of the overall composition of Islam".[1]

He had planned for the second of his ideological trilogy on Islam to be a study entitled "Our Society", but in response to a pressing need that arose then and requests of many readers, as he had declared, he gave preference to publishing a book entitled "Our Economics" to be the second of the series. Sadly, circumstances stood against the publishing of the third part of that series, namely "Our Society". The intellectual arena remained in great expectation and longing for this sequel to be published, but Sayyid as-Sadr was unable to make that work come to light; he went to win martyrdom.

In the introduction to the first edition of "Our Economics", he wrote, " My dear readers. Since we have parted at the time when "Our Philosophy" was published, I said then that it was to be the first part of our Islamic studies, which can be described as a study that deals with the towering Islamic edifice, the edifice of monotheistic faith; after it shall follow studies related to the upper parts of that Islamic edifice; in the end, we shall have a complete picture of Islam, as a lively faith, an overall system of life and a unique program of education and thinking."

We have said this in the introduction to "Our Philosophy", and we expected "Our Society" to be the second study of our research, in which we were to deal with how Islam views man, his social life, his method in analysing and interpreting the social complex, that would take us in the end to the third stage (study), to the Islamic systems of life related to Islam's social thoughts and based upon its ever-fixed edifice of faith.

---

(1) "Our Economics ", Introduction to 1st edition, p. 35, 16th printing

However, incessant requests of readers made us delay " Our Society " and start publishing " Our Economics " as they were in a hurry for a detailed study from the economics of Islam, its philosophy, outlines and teachings".[1]

Interruption of this series that ended with the publication of "Our Economics" by no means signified the cessation of the intellectual writings of Martyr Imam as-Sadr. During the period since "Our Economics" was published till his martyrdom, a considerable number of highly important intellectual writings were published by him, such as the 'Interest-free Banking in Islam', 'Lectures in the Science of *Usool* (principles of jurisprudence)', '*Al-Fatawa Al-Wadhiha* - the Manifest Edicts and the 'Logical Principles of Induction'. This last work is considered among the great works of human thinking in the twentieth century, and the most important in the field of the philosophical and logical thinking. In this work, Sayyid as-Sadr outlined the basis for what he called, "The Theory of Subjective Logic", which reveals "the logical basis for inductive positivism".   On the one hand, this theory analyses inductive positivism and reveals the logical differences between it and evidential positivism. On   the   other   hand,   it   deals philosophically with inductive positivism and outlines the basis upon which this positivism stands as well as the logical rules upon which it is built. With this work of the Martyr Imam, the reign of Aristotelian logic over Islamic philosophical thinking came to an end. There started a new era of Islamic philosophy, largely shorn of Aristotle's logic. When signs of the Islamic Revolution's victory were looming in the horizon of Iran, Sayyid as-Sadr began a series of intellectual works that deal with contemporary social issues and suggest Islamic solutions for them. Most important of these was the treatise   for the

---

(1) Ibid, p.27-28, 16th edition

constitution of the Islamic Republic in Iran; it was of great use for the learned scholars, of the first Iranian Council of Experts, who were elected by the people to codify the Islamic constitution.

One of the most important aspects of creativity in the school of Sayyid as-Sadr is the introduction of a comprehensive change in the classical Islamic studies. The novel drive was started by his school of thought, especially in juridical studies, as well as the studies of the principles of jurisprudence *(usooli)*; the change entailed the content and methodology. This innovative approach is a milestone in the history of this field of knowledge as a whole. Sayyid as-Sadr has established a new school of thought that is characterized by coherence of a curriculum, consolidation of content, depth of thinking and constructive and creative criticism.

The new Islamic thinking brought forth by the genius of the Imam as-Sadr, whether at the level of the new Islamic culture, or at the level of classical studies, has created a strong ideological wave that gradually dominated the intellectual landscape in various Islamic countries, especially Iraq and Iran. This new Islamic thinking had a great effect on immunizing the Muslim cultural mind against foreign ideological invasions, and in the preparation of a suitable ground for an organised political action aiming at attaining an Islamic society based on an Islamic system and tenets of the Holy Qur'an.

The Islamic movement developed along the ideological lines of the school of thought of Sayyid as-Sadr. That is, from the passive (emotional) stage. During this time, the movement was trying with great effort to stop the foreign ideological onslaught and cure the cultural and ideological ailments that became epidemic amongst the circles of Muslim intellectuals as a result of creeping foreign culture into the very fabric of our scientific institutions and cultural organisations. It developed into a new stage in which Islamic ideology was brought to the front lines, armed with the theorisations of Imam as-Sadr, as a strong and active giant chasing the invading ideology right inside its fortifications and institutions, after it had closed the road in front of its attempts for influence and domination over the institutions of thought and culture in the Islamic lands as well as the minds of its men.

Martyr Sayyid as-Sadr undertook a unique leading role in revolutionising the Islamic situation in Iraq, educating its activist generations and directing them both intellectually and politically. He played a pivotal role in educating the Islamic cultural cadre and elements of the Islamic movement and establishing the activist Islamic organisation; he guided its development and ensured its right direction. He also played a leading role in activating and energising the Islamic seminaries - ideologically and politically. Strongholds of the new ideological and political activity were inside the seminaries of Najaf Holy City in particular and in Iraq in general. Of these are, The League of *Ulema* (scholars), The Literary League, Islamic Sciences School, Publishing Forum, Imam al-Jawad Schools, The Administrative Corps of the Supreme Religious Authority, the late Imam Sayyid al-Hakim – its cultural, social and political projects, and the Islamic movement with its various leaderships and groupings; all were feeding on his (as-Sadr's) intellectual prowess, and were guided by his directions and guidance.

After the death of the late fighting, yet forbearing Imam Al-Hakim, Sayyid as-Sadr assumed leadership of the Muslim masses in Iraq. He started organising the Religious Authority Apparatus, establishing a religious relations network that connects the popular base with the Religious Authority through

the clergy and the culturally qualified cadres in the towns and
cities. Before assuming the mantle of Supreme Religious
Leader, he had prepared a full treatise on " the properly guided
religious authority",[1] which was the first theoretical work in the
history of the Shia Religious Authority that attempts to
reorganise the apparatus of the religious authority, as well as
making it efficient and forward-looking, through a well-
researched treatise that is comprehensive and inspiring.

The wide spread and huge following of his supreme religious
authority (*marji'yya*) in Shia quarters coincided with the triumph
of the Islamic Revolution in Iran. He was the first to support it
with vigour. Notwithstanding his distinguished leading position,
he considered himself duty-bound, from a religious perspective,
to tow the line of Imam Khomeini and to protect the Islamic
revolution and support it zealously. This stance, he had
bequeathed his students and followers. He reiterated this clearly
in his known address to his students in Iran during the early
days of the victory of the Islamic revolution, which was led by
Imam Khomeini. In that letter, he said, "The duty of each one
of you, and of every individual whose good fortunes lead him
to live in the midst of this pioneering Islamic experience, is to
spare no effort and capability in the service of this experience,
nor should he spare any effort whilst construction for the sake
of Islam is underway. No limit should be imposed on efforts
whilst the banner of the cause is hoisted high by the force of
Islam. This new constructive project is in need of the efforts of
all individuals, no matter how small. It should also be clear that
Sayyid Khomeini's religious authority which has embodied
Islam's hopes in today's Iran – should be embraced, paid

---

(1) Look, Notes on the mentioned treatise, Introduction to part one of
section two of *mabahithil usool* (Research in the Principles of Jurisprudence),
by Ayatollah Sayyid Kadhim al-Ha'iri, a prominent student of Imam as-Sadr

allegiance to and its interests protected; assimilation into its great existence should be at the same measure it does for the sake of its great goal. The good religious authority is not a person, but a goal and path. Any religious authority that attains that goal is a good one, in which case it should be served with all devotion. The arena of religious authority in Iran should be kept outside all that which may weaken, or does not contribute to safeguarding, the leading and guided authority". [1]

After victory of the Islamic revolution, Sayyid as-Sadr started to escalate the activities of his Islamic revolutionary movement in Iraq. Through the use of cassette tape recorders, or his lectures and letters, he used to send to his students and representatives in various parts inside and outside Iraq, he began to call upon the Iraqi people to wage an overall Islamic revolution against the Ba'thist domination of power in Iraq. In his calls and letters, he was emphasising the need to revolt in the face of tyrants, and the necessity of working towards the application of Islamic teachings in all Islamic countries, rather in every nook of the earth; he reiterated that it is necessary to sacrifice one's own life for the triumph of the true religion of Islam, and in defending the victimised and the oppressed. He was well known for his last three appeals to the Iraqi people. Here are some passages of these appeals; from his first appeal dated 20 Rajab 1399 HL (1978 CE), "O People of my forefathers! I can assure you that I am with you fully, nor shall I abandon you in your ordeal. I shall sacrifice the last drop to the core. I would like to confirm to those at the helm that the oppression directed against the Iraqi people, through the force of iron and fire, that deprived them of the simplest rights and freedoms in observing their religious rites cannot continue. Nor can it always be handled by force and repression. If force was a

---

(1) Ibid, p. 146.

permanent and decisive remedy, the pharaohs and tyrants would have survived. They stopped broadcasting the 'call for prayer' – and we remained patient; they stopped broadcasting Friday prayer, yet we remained patient; they imposed restrictions on staging commemorative ceremonies for the martyrdom of Imam Hussain (May peace be with him); nevertheless, we showed forbearance; they imposed a siege on mosques and inundated them with their men and spies, yet, we persevered; they launched campaigns aimed at coercing people to join the ranks of their party, yet we remained patient; they said, "It is but a transitional period during which people must be galvanised". Nevertheless, we showed resilience. But until when?! Until when shall this transitional period continue?! If a period of ten years' of absolute rule is not enough to prepare an appropriate atmosphere for the Iraqi people to choose their own way, how long should one wait for that? And if a period of ten years of absolute rule did not allow you, O you who are in power! to convince people to join your party, save coercion, what do you hope for?

He then added, "In the name of the human dignity, I demand the release of those who were arbitrarily arrested, the cessation of summary detention that takes place outside the domain of the judiciary. Lastly, I demand, in the name of all of you and in the name of the values you uphold, to allow the people the opportunity to truly exercise its right in running the affairs of the country by way of holding elections through which a council representing the *umma* (community) could truly emerge.

I know that these demands will cost me dearly, may be my life, but these are not the demands of a person that could die out with his death. They are the yearnings of an *umma*, the will of an *umma*, in whose psyche roams the spirit of Mohammed,

Ali and the chosen descendants of Mohammed and his companions, that will never die".[1]

The second part of his second appeal to the Iraqi people, on 10 Sha'ban 1399 HL (1979 CE), continued thus, "O my Dear Iraqi People! O Muslim masses of Iraq! Who have stood up to protect their religion, dignity, freedom, might, and for all values and ideals you blieve in. O Great *Umma* (Islamic community)! Today you are experiencing hard times at the hands of the assassins and butchers, who are astounded by people's wrath and masses' awakening, after they have chained them with iron and instilled fear and terror in their hearts. The bloodletting villains imagine that they have robbed the masses of their esteem and dignity, stripped them of their great faith, the religion of Mohammed, so as to turn these brave believing millions of proud Iraqi people into toys and tools to manipulate as they wish, into which they feed forcibly the allegiance to Aflaq [the founder and theorist of the Ba'th party] and his likes – agents of missionaries and imperialism – in place of allegiance to Mohammed and Ali (May Allah's prayers and peace be with them). Yet, the masses are always stronger than tyrants, no matter how harsh their tyranny becomes. Thus, the tyrants were surprised to discover that the *umma* still pulsates with life, and still has the ability to say its word. As a result of this stance of the *umma*, the tyrants lashed out at tens of thousands of believers and honest sons of this dignified country, with imprisonment, arrests, torture, and death sentences; in the forefront of these victims were the *mujahideen* elite of the *ulema* (religious scholars) whose news informs of their death one after the other under torture".

---

(1) Introduction to part one of Section II of *Mabahithul Usool* by Ayatollah Sayyid Kadhim al-Ha'iri, a prominent student of Imam as-Sadr, p.92.

He went on to mention, "… and I announce to you, O my sons! That I am determined to tread the path of martyrdom. This, therefore, may be the last that you will hear from me, in that the gates of heaven would open to receive the convoys of martyrs.   Allah shall ordain victory for you. How sweet is martyrdom in whose praise the Messenger of Allah *(s.a.w.)* said: It is a good deed with which no misdeed could prevail, in that through martyrdom, the martyr shall have all his sins forgiven no matter how gross they were. It is the duty of every Muslim in Iraq, and every Iraqi outside Iraq, to do all that is in his capacity – even if it cost them their life - to maintain *jihad* and struggle in order to shrug this nightmare off the chest of Iraq, to liberate it from the hands of the inhuman gang, and to establish an honest unique and good rule of government that is based on Islam.   May Allah's peace and blessings be with you".[1]

In his last appeal, whose date is unknown, he said, "O my dear people of Iraq! O You Great *Umma*, In this hard turbulent moment and juncture of your jihad, I would like to address all groupings and sects, Arabs and Kurds alike, Sunni and Shia alike, because the calamity which has been inflected upon us know neither a sectarian, nor ethnic divide; the calamity is universal.   Therefore, the fighting stand, heroic retaliation, and cohesion should be the living reality of all the Iraqi people. From a position of responsibility in this *umma*, I have spared no effort to sacrifice my well-being for the sake of the Shia and the Sunni in equal measure, and for the sake of the Arab and Kurd equally.   This stems from my belief in defending the Message that unites them all, and the faith that unites them all. I have lived my existence for nothing other than Islam, which is the road to salvation and the goal of all. I am with you, O my

---

(1) Ibid, p. 150.

Sunni brother and son, just as much I am with you, O my Shia brother and son! I am with you both in the same measure you are with Islam, and in just as much as you bear of this great flame to salvage Iraq and rid it of the nightmare of oppression, subservience and persecution. The despotic regime (*taghut*) and its followers try to suggest to our noble Sunni sons that it is a matter of Shia and Sunni, so as to separate Sunni from their real struggle against the common enemy. I want to say to you, O sons of Ali and Hussain! and sons of Abu Bakr and Omar! The fight is not between Shia and Sunni rule.

Ali unsheathed his sword in defence of the Sunni rule represented by the Guided Caliphs, which was based on Islam and justice, as he fought as a soldier during the wars waged against the apostates [in the aftermath of the death of the Prophet] under the standard of the first Caliph Abu Bakr. All of us should fight for the banner of Islam to be hoisted high, and under the banner of Islam, no matter what colour was its proponent. The Sunni rule that was bearing the flag of Islam had won the *fatwa* of the Shia clergy, half a century ago, of the necessity to wage jihad for it. Hundreds of thousands of Shia marched out and had sacrificed their lives unselfishly for the sake of safeguarding the standard of Islam, and in order to protect the Sunni rule that was based on Islam. This present *de facto* rule is not a Sunni rule, even though the domineering group is historically related to Sunnism".

He went on to stress, "O my sons and brothers! Do you not see that they have overlooked the religious ceremonies that Ali and Omar defended?! Do you not see that they have swamped the country with wine and pig farms, and all means of impudence and corruption that Ali and Omar together had fought against?! O brothers and sons in Mosul and Basra, in Baghdad, Kerbala and Najaf, in Samarra' and Kadhimiyya, in

Amara, Kut and Sulaimaniyya, sons of Iraq everywhere! I pledge to you that I am for all of you and for the sake of all of you. You are my goal in the present and the future, let your word unite, your ranks consolidate under the banner of Islam, and for the salvation of Iraq from the nightmare of this ruling clique. This would in turn translate into practical steps to building a noble and free Iraq that is filled with the justice of Islam, where dignity of man prevails, and all citizens of different ethnic and religious backgrounds feel that they are brothers. Where all citizens participate in the management of their country, the building of their homeland, and march towards the achievement of their high Islamic ideals that emanate from our Islamic Message, the dawn of our great history. May peace and blessings be with you".

Rumours in Iraq abound that Martyr as-Sadr was planning to leave Iraq. Delegations to show support, solidarity and allegiance started converging on his residence in the Holy City of Najaf, calling on him to remain in Iraq. This was tantamount to a popular mobilisation to prepare the Iraqi people in its confrontation with the regime on one the hand, and demonstrate the influence the Martyr could exert on the populace before the very eyes of the regime on the other hand; however, Sayyid as-Sadr saw fit to stop the march of the delegations so as to prepare other steps for a revolutionary movement which he was equipping the *umma* (Islamic community) for.

The Ba'thist authorities arrested Sayyid as-Sadr on the seventeenth of Rajab 1399 HL (1978 CE). His arrest triggered a big popular uprising in the Holy City of Najaf, led by his sister, Bintulhuda which had culminated in armed confrontation between the masses and the regime's security forces. This uprising was accompanied by other popular protests in major

Iraqi cities, such as Basra, Diyala, Kadhumiyya and others which brought pressure to bear on the regime to temporarily release Sayyid as-Sadr.

On witnessing this popular rallying in support of martyr Imam As-Sadr, which prevented it from eradicating him, the Ba'thist regime resorted to a new plan in its confrontation with the Martyr Imam. It laid seige to the house where he used to live, virtually placing him under house arrest, and preventing the faithful and the *ulema* (religious scholars) from making contact with him. The regime succeeded in its plan.

This situation had continued right up to the time when he was last arrested on 19 Jamad Al-ula 1400 HL (1979-80 CE)., which was followed by arrest of his aggrieved sister Bintulhuda. The malicious Ba'thist authorities murdered the Imam soon after his arrest on that date. He returned unto his Lord as a *mujahid* and martyr, with forbearance and anticipating the good rewards of Allah, may He be pleased with him.

« *Chapter Two* »

Project for Change of Martyr Imam as-Sadr

The period that witnessed the rise of the star of Imam as-Sadr in the skies of the Islamic world was accompanied with the peak of the counter challenges the Islamic existence was made to face, ideologically, politically and socially. On the one hand, atheist ideological currents had begun their onslaught to winning recruits among the intellectuals and university goers. On the other hand, political organisations with leanings to foreign domination on Islamic countries were fast swallowing the active forces of the sons of Islam, and recruiting from them armies of volunteers, highly qualified and capable, slavishly serving foreign powers, the enemies of the Islamic *umma* (community). Thus, the faithful sons of Islam began to feel as outsiders amongst their own people, and estranged though they are in their own country, and in the lands upon whose soil they were born and from its yield they were nurtured. Thus, the transformation project of martyr Imam as-Sadr consisted of three parallel lines:

1. Ideological Change

Martyr Imam as-Sadr realized that the Islamic ideological arena was witnessing an unprecedented challenge from atheist and materialistic ideological schools and trends. This called for a new kind of effort in confronting this counter ideological attack. An overall fundamental change of methods, means and approaches, as well as a new kind of confrontation that would tip the balance of struggle in favour of Islamic ideology, as a faith and as a system, were needed. The aim was to extricate the ideological and spiritual state from the feeling of defeatism and collapse that was dominating the mentality of the Islamic world as a result of its confrontation with Western ideology. This was capable of restoring the state of cohesion and readiness to effectively confront and attack the opposing ideological trends and defeat them in favour of the Islamic ideology that occupies its appropriate position in the world of culture and thought; moreover, to enable it to occupy the throne of ideological leadership of contemporary human society. Thus, Sayyid as-Sadr, has built his project for ideological change upon the following foundations:

a)   Renewing Islamic ideology in a manner that is capable of keeping its originality that stems from the Holy Qur'an and the *sunna* (tradition) of the Prophet. The plan was to present it in a way that is compatible with the requirements of present day life, and meeting the needs of contemporary man as well as proposing appropriate solutions for the problems he faces.

b)   Renewing research and curricula in theology schools (*hawza 'ilmiyya*) and Islamic studies institutions and developing scientific research in the scholastic religious studies which would make them responsive, both in essence and form, to the aspirations and requirements of both contemporary man and society.

c)   Portraying Islam as a comprehensive and harmonious system, which emanates from a deep-rooted philosophical vision for man and universe, augmented by a philosophical proof and logical evidence. There is yet another aspect, i.e. emphasizing the independence of Islam's school of thought, and avoiding the emotional method in the Islamic manner of address which is characterized by the defeatists and those dazzled by Western civilization and its culture; those who never shy away from trying to interpret Islam's tenets and modify them so as to tailor them in harmony with the principles of Western ideology, and make them prisoner to the framework of Western civilisation, values and culture.

d) Confronting the counter ideologies in an objective manner that would reveal, by way of research and deductive logical dialogue, the unsound basis they stand on, their inherent contradictions and impotence to come up with sound solutions for the ailments and problems besetting humanity.

e) Preparing an active generation of intellectuals, from within the ranks of religious scholars and university students, with a view to keeping such intellectuals abreast with Islamic culture and new Islamic thinking, and pushing them to the forefronts of ideological confrontation with the adverse atheist and materialistic ideologies.

2. Social Change

Imam as-Sadr saw that change of the social status in which the *umma* (Islamic community) lives can be achieved only through a leadership that the *umma* trusts, on the one hand, and enjoys the qualifications that enable it to change the social status to the one that is aspired to, on the other. Also such leadership should possess the means that would equip it to introduce this change, on a third level. In the social complex of the *umma* there is no apparatus to be found that is equipped with these skills, other than the apparatus of the religious authority (*al-Marji'yya*), which is the pulsating heart of the *umma* and the hub of religious work and social activity. Yet, the state of individualism, and improvised and primitive state that was governing the prevailing religious authority *(marji'yya)* stood against its occupying an active and leading role within the *umma's* circles. It was imperative, therefore, to begin the process of social change within this pivotal apparatus, and turn it from an individualistic apparatus into an objective organisation through which the religious authority could exercise a leading role, especially in the transformation process. In his treatise for the "objective religious authority", Sayyid as-Sadr wrote:

> *"What distiguishes the good religious authority (marji'yya) most is the adoption of real goals towards which it aims to proceed in the service of Islam. It should possess a clearly defined picture of these goals; thus, it could be considered a clearly guided and conscious marji'yya that always acts on the basis of these goals, instead of acting in a haphazard way, driven by a splintered spirit, and dictated under the spur of the moment of newly arising situations. Based on this, the good religious authority (marji') could offer new results in the service of Islam and bring, into the realm of reality, the best changes for the good of Islam in all situations across the domain of his, i.e. marji', influence and authority".* [1]

Imam as-Sadr saw as among the most important qualities to be possessed by the good *"marji'yya"* are (a) consciousness of its goals; (b) serious adoption of these goals and rapid striving towards achieving them; and (c) following a methodical and practical steps that ensure the achievement of these goals. Defining the goals of the good *marji'yya* in five points, he wrote:

a) Spreading Islam's tenets, on the widest scale possible, amongst Muslims, and working towards providing each

---

(1) Introduction to part one of Section II of *Mabahithul Usool* by Ayatollah Sayyid Kadhim al-Ha'iri, a prominent student of Imam as-Sadr, p.92.

would ensure their commitment to these tenets in their personal conduct.

b)   Creating a wide ideological base within the *umma* (community) that encompasses conscious Islamic understanding, such as the understanding that reiterates that Islam is a comprehensive and complete system for all aspects of life, and taking all measures possible to instill such readily recognized ideas in the minds of Muslims.

c)   Satisfying the Islamic ideological needs necessary for the Islamic action, by way of creating sufficient Islamic research in various economic and social fields, and comparative studies between Islam and the rest of the social doctrines; the enlargement of the scope of Islamic religious jurisprudence is also called for in a manner that enables it to permeate all aspects of life; this in turn calls for developing theology schools (*hawza*) across the board to bring them to the level of shouldering such great tasks.

d)   Guardianship of Islamic works, and supervision of concepts put forward by those working for the cause of Islam in various parts of the Islamic world, with a view to supporting what is right of these concepts and putting right what was wrong.

e)   Bestowal of the title of (leader of the *umma*) on religious scholars, starting from the supreme religious authority (*marji'*) down to the lowest levels of the *ulema*. This, however, should not be seen as a forgone honour, rather by virtue of the *ulema's* adopting the *umma's* interests, being concerned with people's affairs and guarding them, and embracing those working for the cause of Islam.[1]

---

(1) bid, p. 93

He saw that even though the religious authority's (*marji'yya*) consciousness of its goals was the first condition for the attainment of a good religious authority, yet this is not enough for such a *marji'yya* to arrive at its goals. Rather, the practical execution of these goals requires it to take the following two steps:

1. An advance practical preparation; he explained this by saying, "As for the idea of preparatory work that precedes the setting up of the good *marji'yya*, it means that the starting growth of such a *marji'yya* that bears the aforesaid goals requires the presence of a base within Islamic seminaries *(hawza)* and the *umma* (community), which have believed - in one way or the other - in these goals, and to have it ideologically and spiritually prepared in order to contribute to the service of Islam and the establishment of the good supreme religious authority ". [1]

    He also said, "It is indispensable for anyone anticipating to lead the development of the *marji'yya* into a good one to exercise this preparatory work to some extent. This lack of exercise is what made a number of good religious scholars (*ulema*), upon assuming their responsibilities – and in spite of their capabilities - feel totally incapacitated to make changes, since they did not exercise this fundamental work, nor did they define in advance the rational goals for the *marji'yya* and the base that believes in these goals". [2]

2. Development of the approach of *marji'yya* (religious authority) : It is imperative to develop the *marji'yya*

(1) and (2) Ibid, p. 93

organization and to transform its practical mechanisms into active ones that are capable of executing the tasks of the *marji'yya* apparatus and achieving its goals. This can only be done by developing the *marji'yya*'s organization in two spheres:

a) A private sphere, dealing with improving the management corps of the *marji'yya* from within by reorganising it by way of introducing both planning and executing arms that are based on competence, specialisation, division of work and assimilation of all the guided *marji*'s (religious authority) work in the light of the defined goals. Such an organization will replace the entourage of the traditional apparatus of the *marji'yya*. The revamped organization should comprise the following committees:

i A committee charged with supervising the situation/affairs within the religious schools and groups of scholars, developing it in line with the defined objectives of the good *marji'yya* and the running of its administration.

ii A committee for religious science works whose duties are to establish specialised scientific offices charged with carrying out research, follow up of their progress and supervision of Islamic scholarly research, its encouragement and making it subservient to the defined goals.

iii A committee for handling the affairs of religious scholars (*ulema*) in the regions of the country.

iv   A liaison committee responsible for building bridges between the *marji'yya* and the regions that are not yet connected with the management of the religious authority as well as extending a hand to the intellectuals and scholars in the rest of the Islamic world.

v   A committee responsible for sponsoring Islamic action, and offering it support, in various parts of the Islamic world.

vi   A Finance committee that supervises the organisation of financial matters, their administration, and expansion of financial resources.

b) The general sphere; this could materialise in creating a real horizontal extension to the religious authority (*marji'yya*) that would make it an energetically strong magnet towards which all energies and forces associated with the *marji'yya* the world over should be galvanised; this could be achieved through the formation of a council that includes Shia scholars and authorities that religiously represent the supreme religious authority (*marji'*). This council is to include the committees that constitute the *marji'yya*'s administrative arm, where the supreme religious authority (*marji'*) exercises his leadership assisted by this council and its counsel. In addition to its consultative role, the council undertakes responsibility of collaborating with the *marji'yya* in the carrying out of its directives and achievement of its goals"[1]. As such, the good *marji'yya* shall be able to carry out the leading role required of it and through which the required change for the better in the *umma* (community) would be achieved, and which in turn would materialize the

---

(1) Ibid p. 96

sought after goals of Islam.

3. Political Change

Imam as-Sadr saw that the process of overall transformation of the *umma* could be achieved only through the application of Allah's *shari'a* law, in full and in all fields of human activity, which requires the establishment of an Islamic state that is capable of applying Islam in all aspects. Thus, it is essential to prepare the *umma* ideologically and practically in the political arena. As for the ideological preparation, this could be achieved through the dissemination of Islamic political awareness amongst its members; Sayyid as-Sadr reaffirmed the necessity for this Islamic political awareness; he defined it thus, "... Islam has carried this torch flooding with light after mankind had attained a certain degree of awareness, it (i.e. Islam) set out to propagate its moral and ethical message on a wider scale and farther afield; it has hoisted the banner of humanity and built an ideological state that took hold of the world's reins for a quarter of a century; it aimed at uniting all mankind on one ideological platform that profiles both life's pattern and system. The Islamic state has two duties; (a) to groom man upon the ideological base, and make him tailor his own orientations and senses in the same tinge; (b) to monitor him from the outside, and to bring him back to base, should he deviate markedly. Hence, political awareness of Islam is not only an awareness of the formal side of social life, but rather a deep political awareness that is attributable to an overall and complete outlook towards life, universe, society, politics, economics and ethics; this overall outlook is the complete Islamic awareness, and any other political awareness is either a superficial political one that does not look at the world from a certain angle, and does not evaluate its conceptions on a special point of reference, or one that studies the world from a purely materialistic angle that inflicts humanity with conflict and suffering of various forms and kinds ". [1]

An important item of Islamic political awareness is necessity for the establishment of an Islamic state, since it is the Martyr Imam as-Sadr reaffirmed this fact by saying, "The only path for the application of Islam in all life's affairs, the Islamic state is studied once as a religious law (*shari'a*) necessity, for it is the establishment of Allah's rule on earth, and the embodiment of man's role as successor to Allah's will, and once it is studied in the light of this fact, but from the aspect of its great cultural connotations and huge capabilities that distinguishes it from any other social experiment". He went on to say, "The Islamic state is not only a religious law "*shar'iyya*" necessity, but in addition to that a cultural necessity, for it is the only course that is able to harness man's energies in the Islamic world, and elevate him to his natural position on the level of human civilisation, and redeem him from all kinds of suffering - dispersal, subordination and loss". [2]

As for the practical preparation of the Islamic state, this should be accomplished through no less than four projects:

1. Restructuring the religious authority (*marji'yya*) in a manner that would enable it to shoulder the leadership of the *umma* (Islamic community) both ideologically and politically. [3]

2. Cultivating a broad believing popular base that believes in Islam as a true faith; a base that understands this fact a

---

(1) Introduction to "Our Philosophy", p.51-52, 12th edition.
(2) Sources of Islamic Capability, p. 5.

(3) A Treatise on the Good Religious Authority, Introduction to Research in the Fundamentals of Jurisprudence, Sayyid al-Ha'iri, p.93.

conscious understanding, founded on the principle of comprehensiveness in Islam, in that Islam is a complete and comprehensive system for all aspects of life, and that it warrants man's happiness in this life and the hereafter.[1]

However, in cultivating the faithful, stress should be applied on preparing them for sacrifice and steadfastness in the cause of the Islamic leadership goals, leading to the achievement of these goals.

3. Preparing responsible cadres to work amongst the ranks of the *umma* (community) that will rear it up and direct it towards the required political goals.[2]

4. Creating an active Islamic organisation to operate under the supervision of the religious authority *(marji'yya)* that adopts its goals and strives for changing the corrupt political status quo, and achieving the goals of the *marji'yya* on the political level.

In this regard, Martyr Imam as-Sadr set out to establish the Islamic Call *(Da'wa)* Party in Rabi' al-Awal, 1377 HL (1957 CE); he designed a plan of three phases for the party's objectives:

a. Phase of formation of the party, its structuring and the ideological transformation of the umma.

b. Phase of political action, during which the Umma is to be made aware of and acquainted with the Islamic approach adopted by the party, its political stands, and to educate the masses to adopt the party's stands and to protect it.

---

(1) and (2) Ibid, p.93.

c. Phase of ascension to power.

d. A fourth phase was added to the above three, namely the phase _ of safeguarding the interests of Islam and the Islamic *umma* (community), after ascending to power.

Imam as- Sadr saw that the conditions   of the brutal political especially Iraq, make it necessary to merge phases one and two and tyranny that govern some of the Islamic countries, work on both the levels within one phase.

« *Chapter Three* »

Outstanding Achievements of
Martyr Imam as-Sadr

Although genius and innovation in the world of thought
require total mental concentration and keeping away from all
that which may distract the attention and spiritual tranquillity -
in view of the dominant contradiction between the creative
mental outcome and the revolutionary activity in the field - yet
we find the rare ability which characterised the person of our
paradigm Imam as-Sadr has managed to solve this
contradiction. The prolific mental creativity and the
comprehensive theoretical innovation, which the genius of the
Martyr Imam had produced, qualified him to occupy a unique
role on the level of pioneering ideology of contemporary
Islamic awakening.[1]

Yet, all of that did not prevent him from leading the people's
revolutionary activity in the real world. Although the area that
he was destined to exercise his pioneering political role in was
limited to Iraq, yet his pioneering role, whether on the
ideological and theoretical levels, or on the real ground and
application level, was not confined to the boundaries of a
certain country or a specific area; rather, it extended to all
Islamic lands and even surpassed it to cover the Islamic
communities all over the world.

Hereunder, we shall summarise the major achievements of
the Imam as-Sadr, (a) in the ideological field, and (b) on the

---

(1) Ibid, p. 90-91

practical and application level. As for his achievements in the ideological level, those could be summarised in the following points:

1. His creativity in the techniques of methodical research in Islamic studies.

The most significant characteristic of Imam as-Sadr's ideology is his unique logical methodology that is seldom to be found in men of thought and scientific research. Sayyid as-Sadr possessed an organised methodical thinking that does not deal with an idea without forming it in a co-ordinated logical mould. You often find him dealing with an idea, that he sets out to discuss and criticise, yet imparting on it an evidential form and a uniform methodical style to explain it even better than its original proponent. The main points of the methodical innovation in the thinking of the Martyr as-Sadr could be summarised as follows:

a) A comprehensive uniform vision towards the heritage of the revelation, which strives to present Islam as an overall system, whether in its faith fundamentals or juridical structure.

b) Discovery of the inductive subjective logic, which he expounded in his book " The Logical Principles of Induction ", and its employment in religious research, in addition to the evidential syllogism logic.

c) Clarity of expression, beauty of composition, exactitude in performance and proportionality in literary and logical terms.

d) Logical analysis of the idea into its components and composites and exposition of the interrelationships between them.

e) Disentanglement of complex subjects and lending each constituent part its logical share of study.

f) Investigating the probabilities of research and giving due consideration to possible hypotheses at the level of scientific study and research.

g) Arranging the points and subjects of research in a manner that places each one of them in its appropriate logical sequence.

2. Studying the other idea and challenging it logically in the field of scientific research.

Although scholastic research in Islamic institutes of learning and religious schools has known scientific dialogue since the dawn of scientific activity in the first *Hijri* [lunar] century, a matter which men of science and thought are still practising, keeping abreast with works of other schools of thought, where they study and criticise scientific works, yet we find the attempt, undertaken by the late Professor Imam as-Sadr, in studying ideological works of other schools, which manifested itself vividly in his two books "Our Economics" and "Our Philosophy", unique in its kind and unknown before by the institutions of Islamic learning. This is true of both the depth and universality, on the one hand, and its method and style on the other. What distinguishes the school of Professor as-Sadr in this field could be summarised by the following:

a) Depth in contemplating the other idea and infinite exactness in studying and presenting it.

b) Extensive and comprehensive research into what is put forth by the other schools of thought, whether in the area of lively dialogue, in the field of theoretical research, or in the real world of practical application.

c) Solid objective logical style in studying the other idea that keeps the researched subject away from all that which may disturb the realm of logical contemplation, such as resorting to taunting and mockery tactics, sharp criticism methods, or the like.

d) Documenting scientific research and largely depending upon accredited references in studying the other idea.

e) Superiority of logic, emanating from superior scientific ability, which equipped him to challenge the other idea in a fight that did not leave it any escape route but to concede defeat and surrender.

3. Handling contemporary problems and issues faced by man.

The ideological achievements of Imam as-Sadr are characterized by their serious tone and focus on the issues facing contemporary man, and the proposition of modern Islamic solutions for them. Each one of such works, like Our Economics, Our Philosophy, Interest-free Banking in Islam, Islam Leads Life, The Manifest Edicts, Lessons in the Science of the Principles of Jurisprudence, The Logical Principles of Induction, and other major intellectual achievements, addresses either a general contemporary problem, or a special one that is experienced by a particular section of society; he also saw that such problems have a bearing on the present and the future of the *umma*.

4.   Scientific innovation in the field of Islamic studies.

Martyr Imam as-Sadr practised critical editing of texts in the field of higher studies in the University of Holy Najaf for a period of more than a quarter of a century. He contributed to the ideological output in the most important fields of Islamic knowledge, especially philosophy, jurisprudence (*fiqh*) and principles of jurisprudence (*usool*). His scientific work in those fields stands out as comprehensive, thorough, and innovative. He managed to decipher the heritage of learned men passed and fathom the thoughts of contemporaries. He went on to develop what he found deserving as such and criticised what he saw as point of contention. So immense was his success in these fields that an aggregate of his works and thought have brought into being a distinctive and new school distinguished for its investigative examination, creative opinion and new methodology. Martyr as-Sadr had his own school of thought that integrates philosophy, religious jurisprudence and principles of jurisprudence. In my own opinion, the depth and novelty of ideas which the Martyr Imam had put forth - especially in comparison to the traditional way of thinking that characterised Islamic studies for long - have caused a kind of deceleration in the permeation of his ideas through the mentality of classical religious institutions and delayed their dominance in the arena of higher Islamic studies. However, his ideas have begun to occupy large areas of the thinking of the religious intelligentsia; no doubt, the future will witness the dominance of as-Sadr school of thought, with its ideas and innovative approach, in the world of mind and thought within the circles of Islamic seminaries and higher study institutions.

It is inopportune in this hasty dispatch to present, even in a quick glance, the features of the new thinking that the school of Martyr Sayyid as-Sadr has created in various fields of Islamic knowledge. We had presented an overall picture, of the features of his new fundamentalist school, in our treatise entitled "Features of the New Fundamentalist Thinking", which is an abridged study of the features of fundamentalist thinking of Imam as-Sadr compared with the fundamentalist school of ash-Sheikh al-Ansari. We hope that researchers and text editors would carry out comparative in-depth studies of as-Sadr's prolific works, that straddle all spheres of Islamic knowledge. Then the greatness of the ideological achievements of Martyr as-Sadr would become evident to researchers; its extensiveness, depth and effect in structuring the new Islamic thought would also become manifest.

The most important of his practical achievements can be summarised thus:

a) Nurturing highly moralistic cadres, armed with knowledge, both inside and outside the Islamic seminaries. This has had a great impact on guiding the Islamic movement, educating and directing the *umma*'s various sections.

b) Insulating the minds of Muslim intellectuals from the onslaught of Western atheist ideology. That is, in spite of what this ideology had equipped itself with of elements of temptation and influence, such as its huge media empire that swept the world East and West, and its scientific and technological capabilities that are dominating the world capitals, and virtually affecting the political process and decision-making. That is, it holds sway over scientific and cultural institutions, let alone the huge financial temptations and economic clout that facilitate its influence and achieving its objectives.

c) Establishing the Islamic activist organisation, which is considered a qualitative step in the history of Islamic resurgence within the Shia domain.

d) Setting up the administrative arm of the guided religious authority (*marji'yya*), on the lines discussed in his treatise on "the good religious authority". However, the period of his holding the title of "religious authority" did not last long, i.e. not more than ten years, considering that his wide reputation did not gather momentum only in the last five years that preceded his martyrdom, neither did it spread wide enough to enable him to achieve the goals he set out to achieve; that was due to the presence of competing religious authorities that are deep rooted, with large following and long existence, which, of course, were attempting not to let his religious authority (*marji'yya*) gain any wider following; that was coupled with what the ruling Ba'th regime in Iraq was exercising, of various means of pressure and attempts to hinder his religious authority, so as not to allow it to spread amongst the ranks of the populace (*umma*); among these tactics was arresting his representatives in different parts of the country, and imposing severe surveillance upon those cooperating with his religious authority or connected to it.

e)   Setting forth the Islamic revolution in Iraq, leading it from the front, and ensuring its continuity through his great and heroic steadfastness in the face of ferocious tyrants unto martyrdom.

Phase III

The Revolution

and

Establishing the State

The Revolution and
Establishing the State

No doubt, the *umma* (Islamic community) – and any nation for that matter – cannot ascertain its existence in the real world, without having its own integral political entity that represents its will, embodies its identity and realizes its values and ideals, and protects its interests.

Even though Muslims constitute an *umma* that bears all the characteristics of one nation from a historical viewpoint, yet from not so long a period of time gradually began to lose elements of its identity. Instead, it has turned into splinter groups that are united by no more than a heartfelt faith in Islam and some aspects of its acts of worship, which in turn have lost their social and political content, and turned into traditions that Muslims got accustomed to performing, in as much as others got accustomed to other customs and habits. And here comes the great importance of the Islamic revolution led by Imam Khomeini, where for the first time in our new and near epoch, it has restored, to Muslims, their identity, breathed new life into the Islamic body, hence the resurrection of the Islamic *umma* (community); suddenly the scattered Islamic existence, which was lost in the midst of eastward and westward tumultuous currents, has transformed into an actively symmetrical Islamic existence on the ground that knows itself and believes in its goals and values.

The Islamic *umma* was reborn when Imam Khomeini carried the banner of Islamic revolution and led the Muslim Iranian people – who represented the Islamic *umma* with all its values and aspirations – in confronting powers of arrogance in all its weight, hardware and armies, till Providence granted him victory in full and new horizons opened up. Banners of atheism and unbelief that were raised by the stooges of the world imperialistic powers in Iran were finally lowered and folded; in their place was raised the banner of the Qur'an and Islam. The late Imam Khomeini established a modern state based on the foundations of the Islamic *shari'a* law and its teachings and tenets. In order to clarify some aspects of this stage of the history of the Islamic awakening, which is considered as the most important and most difficult, and to shed some light on part of the life history of its greatest pioneer Imam Rohullah al-Mosawi al-Khomeini, we shall set our study in four chapters.

« Chapter One »

A Short Biography of
Imam Khomeini

The noble descent of Imam Rohullah al-Mosawi al-Khomeini goes back to Imam Mosa bin Ja'far as-Sadiq, a great grandson of Allah's Messenger, Mohammad, (May peace be with him and his pure descendants). It is for this reason that he was attributed the surname al-Mosawi, the same as other noble *Sayyids*, or Hashimites, related by descent to Imam Mosa bin Ja'far (May Allah's peace be with him).

Imam Khomeini was born on the twentieth of Jamadi ath-Thania, 1320 HL (1902-3 CE) in the City of Khomein, which is one of the towns of Arak Province - in central Iran.

His father, Sayyid Mostafa al-Mosawi, was a prominent religious scholar who was trained in religious knowledge at the hands of the great religious leader at the time, Imam Alhasan ash-Shirazi. After finishing his higher studies in Najaf and Samara, (both in Iraq), he returned to Khomein to replace his father Sayyid Ahmed al-Mosawi, a high-ranking scholar in the city of Khomein.

Sayyid Ahmed Al-Mosawi was a great scholar living in Najaf. The people of the city of Khomein called him to their city so as to guide them and handle their religious affairs; he responded and took leave to Khomein and stayed there.

Sayyid Mostafa al-Mosawi (father of Imam Khomeini) was martyred in the year 1320 HL (1902-3 CE). – the same year that Imam Khomeini was born – on the road between Arak and

Khomein at the hands of outlaws and evildoers. Thus, the newly born Rohullah was destined to be brought up as an orphan, looked after by the Providence and the sympathy of his mother and relatives, especially his aunt (*Sahiba*) who devoted herself to his care and good upbringing.

The Imam took his initial religious education in the city of Khomein from a group of its religious scholars, especially his eldest brother – Sayyid Mortadha Pisindida. After that, he set out for the city of Arak in the year 1339 HL (1920-1 CE) in order to continue his studies there.

At that time, Arak was an important metropolis of knowledge (science) in Iran with a big number of great professors of Islamic sciences and religious scholars (*ulema*), headed by the Shia leader, at the time, Imam Sheikh Abdul-Karim al-Hai'ri.

When Imam Hai'ri made up his mind to set out for Qom in the year 1340 HL (1921-2 CE), he took him (the young Khomeini) along with his entourage, and settled there. He attended Imam Hai'ri's higher studies lectures in jurisprudence (*fiqh*) and principles of jurisprudence (*usool*) until he had attained the level of independent judgement in religious matters (*Ijtihad*). He studied physics and astronomy under the supervision of Sheikh Ali Akbar al-Yazdi; he trained in gnosis (*irfan*) and philosophy at the hands of the Theologian and Great Professor Sheikh Mohammed Ali Shah-Abadi.[1]

Since his early days, Imam Khomeini took great interest in training his soul and purifying it. In his boyhood, he was deeply

---

(1) Sayyid Hameed Rohani, *Barresi va Tahlili az Nehzat-e Imam Khomeini*, (Studies and Analysis of Imam Khomeini's Uprising) vol. 1, p.27

committed to the principles of morals; he was observant of Islamic manners, and ascetic in his life. He was keen on remembering and mentioning Allah in all circumstances, keeping vigil and reclusive to his religious duties, humble and sedate; He does not deviate from the lifestyle of the pious, nor disposition of the good, keeping away from idle talk, silent except in what pleases Allah of a conversation relating to knowledge or praise to Allah with reverence, or a discussion that leads to the settling of an issue or guidance. Since his early days, he was an example of high morals, virtue and piety. He achieved the prominence the scholars in the Islamic seminary of the Holy City of Qom usually enjoy. He played the role of the good educationalist and self-possessed teacher, embarking on lecturing ethics alongside other disciplines, such as jurisprudence, principles of jurisprudence and philosophy. Around him gathered those eager to descipline the soul and acquire nobility of character; his lecture circles had, thus, become a congregation of cultured souls and scholars noted for their virtues of knowledge and work.

In addition to lecturing in ethics, he embarked upon lecturing in philosophy. His first lectures in philosophy started in 1347 HL ((1928-9 CE).[1], after which he lent importance to lecturing in gnosis (*irfan*). He also used to lecture in the higher level of jurisprudence and principles of jurisprudence. In 1364 HL (1945 CE), he began lecturing in both the disciplines at the level of external research. His diligent students wrote much of

---

(1) My father related to me that he had attended Imam Khomeini's lectures in the explanation of *Mandhoomat as-Sabzwari*. This seems to have been around 1350 HL (1931-2 CE). – before my father was set to leave to the Holy City of Najaf, Iraq. At that time, Imam Khomeini was one of the outstanding professors of philosophy in the theology schools (*hawza*) of Qom, according to what my father had told me.

his research work in the said two disciplines. Of these, Ayatollah Sheikh Mujtaba at-Tehrani's transcriptions in jurisprudence and Ayatollah Sheikh Ja'far as-Subhani's transcriptions in principles of jurisprudence, are noted. As such, Imam Khomeini proceeded in his efforts to educating religious scholars *(ulema)* and refining the souls until his classes achieved wider acclaim in Qom. Imam Khomeini became Qom's leading professor for education and learning.[1] The number of students, graduated from his classes, who had attained the level of independent judgement in matters of religious practice *(ijtihad)* reached more than five hundred jurists *(faqih)*.[2]

Many of his works, in various disciplines of Islamic knowledge, have been published. Of these are the following:

1. The Lantern of Guidance – Gnosis *(irfan)*.

2. Explanation of the "Morning *(Sahar)* Supplication"- Gnosis.

3. The Forty Traditions – Morals and gnosis.

4. Commentary on *Fusus al-Hikam* (Gems of Wisdom)– Gnosis.

5. Commentary on the "Key to the Unknown" – Philosophy and gnosis.

6. Secrets of Prayer - or "The Ascension of the Good" - Morals and gnosis.

---

(1) Sayyid Hameed Rohani, *Barresi va Tahlili az Nehzat-e Imam Khomeini*, (Studies and Analysis of Imam Khomeini's Uprising) vol. 1, p.51 and following.
(2) Ibid, p. 42.

7. A Treatise on "Request and Will" – Philosophy and principles of jurisprudence.

8. Commentary on the explanation of *Ra's al-Jalut* tradition by al-Qadhi Sa'eed. He also explained it separately.

9. Revealing the Evildoers – Speculative theology.

10. Explanation of the Prophetic Tradition regarding "soldiers" of reason and ignorance – Morals and gnosis.

11. Ethics of Prayer – Morals and gnosis.

12. The Epistles - A collection of treatises on the principles of jurisprudence; they include the following: Principle of No-harm, a kind of analogy - (*istishab*), Parity and Preference, Independent Judgement (*ijtihad*) and Emulation (*taqleed*), Dissimulation (*attaqiyya*).

13. *Tahreer al-Waseela* – A Compendium of Religious Edicts.

14. Book of Purity, in three volumes - Deductive Jurisprudence (*fiqh istidlali*).

15. Refining the Science of Principles of Jurisprudence (*tahtheebul usool*), in three volumes – His research in this science is written by his student Sheikh Ja'far as-Subhani.

16. Book of Business (*kitabul bay*'), five volumes, in deductive jurisprudence.

17.   The Islamic Government, A treatise on Islamic government and the guardianship of the jurist, or the jurist-ruler, (*walayatul faqih*).

18.   Illicit Gains, two volumes - Deductive Jurisprudence.

19.   The Greatest *Jihad* (*Al-Jihadul Akbar*) – A report on a lecture on ethics delivered to his students in Najaf, Iraq.

20.   Qur'anic Commentary on the opening Chapter of the Holy Qur'an, *al-Fatiha*.

An Abridged Account of his Political Life

Imam Khomeini embarked on political activity since he was of a tender age. He had kept pace with political events in the world, and Iran in particular. He was following the political discussions that went on inside the peoples *shura* council [Parliament] of Iran in his early teens. He had lived through the political events that occurred in Iran after the constitutional revolution, which ended in Riza Khan's taking the reins of power and the resulting domination of the absolute despotic rule in Iran, accompanied by the policy of estrangement that resulted in an iron-fisted dictatorship based upon suppressing freedoms and suffocating political activity. Those policies included a scheme aimed at total dismantling of religious manifestations in social life. It also resulted in the imposition on women not to dress in *hijab* [Islamic code of dress] and a plan for a uniform dress which prevented Iranians from wearing their national dress; instead Western dress was imposed upon them. Severe restrictions were also imposed on religious scholars (*ulema*) and religious schools (*hawza*), limiting religious activity, banning Hussaini religious ceremonies, and harassing enlightened *ulema* (religious scholars). This repressive course led to violent confrontations between the people and the regime's authorities; most noted of these was the massacre of Gohershad in the city of Mashhad, where Riza Shah's henchmen besieged the masses who gathered inside the mosque and opened fire on them. The outrageous act resulted in tens of casualties, dead and injured. Under the government of his son Mohammed Riza, the Western hegemony, which characterised the reign of Riza Khan, continued. Rather it became severer and developed into a complex form that dominated all aspects of life such as thought, culture, art, literature, politics, and the economy. All of this went on under the harsh conditions of a dictatorial policy that liquidated any opposing voice and banned all political activity that is not subservient to the Shah's will. This repressive policy had imposed, upon the Shah government, a heavy burden that made it set up a huge security apparatus that went on to exercise the most barbaric practices against dissidents and *mujahideen*. Torture, burning, death sentences, imprisonment and the like, are just a few examples of such practices.

The dictatorship of Mohammed Riza reached the peak of its cruelty after the crackdown on the popular uprising, which called for the nationalisation of oil in 1953, led by the religious leader Imam Abulqasim al-Kashani on the popular level, and Dr. Mohammed Musaddaq on the political and international level. The result was that the Shah was forced to flee Iran in its aftermath. But the Iranian army, led by Zahidi, a close associate of the Shah, led a coup d'etat and blockaded residences of the two leaders, Imam al-Kashani and Musadaq, and imposed a house arrest on both of them in around the clock surveillance. The Shah then returned to Iran, relying on a doubly increased American support, after which he embarked upon a new policy that included, in addition to the dictatorial political terror, the starting of construction and economic projects aimed at creating a situation of economic prosperity and development, and raising living standards. This was designed to win the hearts and minds of the population and to ensure the popular support for the government of the Shah, after it had completely lost its popularity because of its repressive practices during the popular uprising that accompanied the oil nationalisation.

Imam Khomeini was watching these events with awareness and vigilance, scrutinising the political movements with a view to fathom their aims. Through analysing these events deeply, he deduced the safest course that ensured success and good fortune for the popular political activity aimed at liberating the country from the dictatorial regime and Western hegemony, and establishing a popular Islamic rule that ensured freedoms and rights for all sections of the *umma* (community).

Through his own personal experience, and close encounters with political events inside Iran and abroad, coupled with his knowledge of the political history of the Islamic *umma* (community), he had concluded that any popular liberation movement inside the Islamic society would not reap good results and success, unless it possessed the following constituents:

1. **Islamisation of the Movement:** This should permeate its ideology, goals and methods, in that as Islam is the catalyst that will bring back to Islamic society its true identity, it ensures the unity of goal and purpose for its social activity and supplies the Islamic political action with the purpose and energy that gives the activists the strength necessary for the steadfastness and resilience to face up to obstacles and problems. It also arms them with the ability to stand

firm in pursuing the goals, emanating from the principles that develop inside them the spirit of altruism, sacrifice, and to die for the cause of Islam.

2. **Popularity of the movement:** The populace interaction with the movement and its goals is one of the basic conditions for the success of the liberation movement.

Wherever it may be, any liberation movement shall often be met with a ferocious tyrannical regime, that has at its disposal financial, political and military means, protected by a web of preparations and capabilities that are merciless and unrelenting; it is, thus, unhindered by any deterrent from committing the most brutal of crimes in order to keep its grip on power. It may as well, resort to the "carrot and stick" policy in furtherance of its objectives and lasting rule and supremacy in the political and social arena. Such despotic regimes spare no effort in using measures and practices in clamping down upon any kind of dissent. In facing up to this type of tyranny, a total popular mobilisation is imperative; a wide and continuous popular interaction becomes vital so as to enable the liberation movement to destabilise the regime and weaken it as a first step, then topple it in order to attain its liberation goals as a second step.

3. **The leadership:** This is the basic constituent for the liberation movement, as it is impossible for the liberation movement to succeed in its aims without having a good leadership that leads its active struggle in the right path. Such leadership is usually equipped with the right qualifications to take the right decision in the event of a confrontation; it should also be capable of rallying popular support for the liberation movement, supply the

movement's activists with the ideas and planning and inspire in them determination, firmness of stand, steadfastness, and arouse in them morals and spiritual prowess that enable them to proceed on the path of achieving the goal of liberation. The leadership cannot attain its goals, if it is bereft of the following two prerequisites:

a) **Scholarly and practical competence.** This means that the leader should be a just jurist (*faqih*), with the traits of a leader that enable him to lead the masses on the path of liberation and, ultimately, the setting up of a just Islamic rule.

b) **Mutual confidence between the competent leader and the masses.** This is required so that the leader inspires confidence in the masses, leading to fluid practice of leadership by the man on the top, on the one hand, and interaction by the masses in obeying his orders and continued support, on the other. The leader should also have trust in his masses and that they are faithful to him along the path of liberation and achievement of his great revolutionary goals.

The political ideology of Imam Khomeini (May his soul rest in peace) had developed upon that basis, as he has established his own political theory on the following premises:

    i. It is imperative that the political movement adopts Islam as a goal, way, faith and system. This is so because Islam is the only revolutionary enterprise that is capable of mobilising the masses in a revolutionary manner that ensures success on the path of liberation, as well as having a system that is suited to managing the human life in a manner that ensures justice, advancement and prosperity for all.

ii. The Islamic movement cannot afford to dispense with the masses. Therefore, it must strive incessantly to secure the support and sympathy of the masses at all the milestones of its course of struggle and political activity.

The Islamic movement should also make use of the means and opportunities that are made available by the popular support.

iii. The Islamic movement should avail itself of a learned just and competent juridical leadership that has the trust of the masses, on the one hand, and in turn the masses have trust in it, on the other.

Based on this, Imam Khomeini had tried, in various periods of time, to initiate his political move, but he did not find the socio-political circumstances suitable to his own revolutionary aspirations, neither could he find the circumstances commensurate to creating the conditions, mentioned above, that are necessary to making the political Islamic move.[1]

Imam Khomeini witnessed three periods of religious leaderships that had succeeded in making strides within Iranian society. The first was the leadership of Imam Abdul Karim al-Ha'iri during the regime of Riza Khan; the second was the leadership of the three highest ranking jurists: Sayyid

(1) Ibid, p.95-112

Mohammed Taqi al-Khonsari, Sayyid Mohammed al-Hujja and Sayyid Sadruddin as-Sadr; and the third was the leadership of Imam Sayyid Hussain al-Brojardi. Least of all that these religious leaderships were suffering from was lack of confidence, on the part of masses, in the leadership's realisation of the goals, and the lending of their unmitigated and continuous support to the leadership in the liberation movement till the achievement of the goal. The harsh experience of the religious leadership during the constitutional movement, which led to the criminal elements attacking members of that leadership, murdering and imprisonment some of its figures - such as the death sentence passed against the great religious leader Sheikh Fadhlollah an-Nouri, the murder committed against the other religious leader Sayyid Hassan al-Mudarris, let alone those who spent their lifetime in exile and prison – and the subsequent collapse of the liberation movement, stagnation of religious activity, increased foreign influence, escalation in the suppression of political and religious activities and the regime's indulgence in its repressive policies. This harsh experience of not so long past had its negative effects, not only on denting the morale of the masses, but also on the religious leadership's confidence in the worthiness of the masses' support and the extent of its readiness to continue lending support to the religious leadership in confronting the dictatorial regime dominating the destinies of the Muslim people in Iran.

Imam Khomeini studied the psychology of the Iranian people, acquainted himself with the points of strength and weakness inherent in this *umma* (community), and believed without any doubt that the religious spirit and moral conditions within the Iranian people were mature, ready for sacrifice and standing fast – especially after what it had suffered during the reigns of the first and second Pahlavi Shahs - which made it ready for a popular uprising that was not likely to subside until it achieved victory, nor would it quiesce till it attained its goals.

He waited for the right opportunity to materialise, an opportunity that constitutes the following elements:

1. That he should avail himself of the opportunity to address the masses as a religious leader whose orders the faithful would respect.

2. That he should have available for him a group of activists amongst religious scholars (*ulema*), theology students, and intellectuals; those should be ready to assume the role of an executive body that directs, guides and monitors the popular movement and steers it towards its defined objectives.

3. An opportune social event that could trigger popular incitement, and raise political awareness of the masses with a view to mobilising them and sharpening their wits against the regime, its media and repressive apparatus.

After the death of Imam al-Brojardi, last of the religious leaders, who had preceded Imam Khomeini in the religious leadership of the Iranian people, Imam Khomeini was acknowledged by the popular circles as a religious leader, meriting to hold the office of "supreme religious authority" - (*marji'yya 'ulia*). On the other hand, a large number of learned religious jurists (*mujtahideen*) and scholars (*ulema*) had graduated from the school of Imam Khomeini; those formed a broad base of learned religious men and cadres who followed the Imam's religious edicts (*fatwa*), political and social opinions, and who were ready to be proponents of his enlightened political thought and achieve his goals. Thus, two elements of the awaited opportunity, which were necessary for Imam Khomeini to kick-start his Islamic and popular revolution, had been made available. There remained the imperative third element, namely the socio-political event which merits the outbreak of an overall popular revolution.

The government of the Shah miscalculated the death of Imam al-Brojardi, of whose religious influence it was fearsome, as a vacuum on the level of the religious leadership – who had a wide popular influence as a golden opportunity to implement its prepared plan. The plan had first aimed at completely dampening the religious spirit and Islamic identity of the Iranian people, and severing its ties with its Islamic past and religious heritage; on a second assumption it had aimed at destroying all that could constitute a source of concern for the government, in that it could have deemed it dangerous to its stability or ability to execute its plans and policies; on a third assumption, it had aimed at Westernising Iran, with a view to wiping out its religious identity, eradicating the roots of its religious sentiments and Islamic leanings, once and for all.

The first step that the government of the Shah had embarked upon in this course of action was its suspension of the national parliament and council of dignitaries, its announcement of the plan for "local committees – law (Qanon-e Anjomanhay-e Iyalati va Velayati), which for the first time had done away with the condition of swearing on the Holy Qur'an by those elected, and had referred to "The Divine Book" instead. It had also cancelled the condition of being Muslim for the voters and candidates. All of this was in a bid to sever the ties of the people with Islam and the Holy Qur'an, efface its religious identity and undermine its faith and cultural character. This would, in their scheme of things, pave the way for the

Zionists, and their lackeys, to manipulate the resources of the Iranian Muslim people and their country's wealth.[1]

Imam Khomeini met with other high ranking doctors of religion in the City of Qom, and explained to them the dangerous plot the Shah government was hatching. He agreed with them on a stand that rejects and condemns the government declaration of the local committee's plan and its cancellation of the condition of both voters and candidates being Muslim, and the cancellation of the swearing upon the Holy Qur'an. Imam Khomeini began issuing statements of condemnations, addressing the people, at some times, and the government, at others. Those calls spread amongst the populace who had manifested an unprecedented response. This was augmented by the support and solidarity shown by the religious fraternity in Qom and Mashhad - and that of their counterparts in Najaf, Iraq - towards Imam Khomeini. It yielded the desired effect on the people's spirit. In one of his messages to the government, Imam Khomeini declared, 'Once again I urge you to submit to Allah, the Most High, and to work in accordance with the constitution. I warn you of the bitter results that you shall reap as a consequence of violating the Qur'an and Islamic dictates delivered by the nation's religious scholars. I warn you against violating the constitution and throwing yourselves into this mined field. Otherwise, Islam's *ulema* shall not hesitate to voice their opinion of you.'[2]

After facing these condemnations and popular rejection, and having witnessed the growing religious and popular opposition, the Shah government backed down and cancelled the planned

---

(1Ibid, p.146-148
(2) *Sahif-e Noor* (The Book of Light), vol.1, p. 15

local committees on 7 Azar, 1341 HS (28 November, 1962 CE). The people of Iran celebrated this day as a great victory for the *ulema*, led by Imam Khomeini. But acting on instructions from the   United States, the government was determined on continuing its plans. On 9.10.1341 HS (9.1.1963 CE), the Shah announced his so-called White Revolution which comprised six points. In so doing, the government was aiming at extending the American domination over the country's political, economic and cultural landscapes. The government of the Shah was trying to carry out this plan under the guise of reform and construction, so as to make it appear to serve the workers and farmers, secure their legitimate rights, and aim at spreading culture and eliminating illiteracy. But in actual fact it was only a plan designed by American policy that would ensure for the United States a lasting domination over Iran, and the extension of its cultural, political and economic influence in this strategic country under the pretext of a reformist project.

The six-point plan announced by the Shah, in what he called the white revolution, were:

1. Abolition of the feudal system on the basis of the agrarian reform law.
2. Nationalisation of forestry and pasture lands.
3. Sale of shares of state companies to support agrarian reform projects.
4. Workers sharing in the profits of plants and factories.
5. Reform of elections law.
6. Establishment of *Sepah-eDanesh*, i.e. the army of science, in order to disseminate compulsory education.

Most dangerous of these were the last two, in that the government was aiming at extending the American domination politically and culturally, along with the remaining points that, in reality, were aimed at extending the American influence in the country economically. When the Shah announced his "white revolution", the religious leadership, headed by Imam Khomeini, rose up to declare its rejection of this so-called revolution in its entirety and detail. In its rejection of the Shah's revolution, it also extended its rejection of his policy of subordination to the United States and support of the Zionist entity. Imam Khomeini managed to garner, to his stand, the support of the majority of religious scholars (*ulema*) in Qom and Mashhad. They all took a united stand against what the Shah had called a white revolution. All in unison, they declared unlawful the participation in the referendum on the Pahlavite revolution which the government had decided to carry out on 6 Bahman 1341 HS, (26 January 1963 CE). On 2 Bahman 1341 HS (22 January 1963 CE), Imam Khomeini issued a statement in which he deemed unlawful the participation in the intended referendum, making it clear to the people that the referendum violates the Iranian constitution, and the interests of the people. He also unveiled the hidden agenda of the government, the dangers that threaten the country's independence, and extension of foreign domination and Zionist influence upon the political, cultural and economic arenas in Iran.

Imam Khomeini's declaration of prohibiting participation in the referendum and his condemnation of the Pahlavite so-called revolution, dubbed by the Shah as the "White Revolution", spread fast amongst the people. The masses were reacting to it in an unprecedented manner. In Tehran, the masses rose up and took to the streets, led by high-ranking clerics, condemning the Pahlavite revolution and the referendum process which the government of the Shah had announced. The bazar (Tehran's central market) announced its full support of the stand of the religious establishment, and called for a general strike; shops and super markets closed their doors in solidarity with the popular uprising led by the *ulema* (religious scholars). Police and the security forces clashed with the masses, who took out to the streets, dispersed them with naked brutality, and managed to clamp down on this popular dissent, but for a while.

This popular solidarity with the *ulema* in their rejection of the Shah's plan dealt the Shah a big blow and scuppered his attempts to impose American cultural and political domination on Iran. It was necessary for the Shah to come up with a step that guarantees, at the least assumptions, the dividing of the religious stand against him, and to ensure for his plan some sort of legitimate support. He decided to visit the city of Qom on 4 Bahman 1341 HS (24 January 1963) in order to meet with its religious scholars and from there he would address the nation to tout the support of the religious establishment for his white revolution; in so doing, he would ensure the people's support for it, and let Imam Khomeini and his colleagues miss the opportunity of inciting the people against his planned revolution. But Imam Khomeini declared his strong opposition towards receiving the Shah, and agreed with the majority of the religious scholars on a complete boycott of the Shah, rejecting to meet with him, come what may. Imam Khomeini passed an edict, deeming unlawful the participation in receiving the Shah; he asked the people to stay at home on the day of the Shah's arrival, and to boycott completely the ceremonies of the reception.

The masses in Qom showed solidarity with their religious scholars by completely boycotting the reception party of the Shah. Shops and markets closed their doors; the people stayed away; the absence of both the clergy and the masses from the party was clearly manifest. Furthermore, the city appeared like a ghost town, except for elements of the security apparatus, police and the military, and a small group of peasants and workers who were forcibly brought by the security forces to participate in the Shah's reception party.

The Shah came to Qom. He was greatly vexed with what he saw of the masses' boycott, had done without the visit normally paid to the tomb of *Sayyida* Ma'soma in Qom, and hurriedly coined the call that he had intended to address the masses with. The call came out trivial. In it, he attacked the religious scholars (*ulema*) of Qom and branded them reactionaries and backward, talked in glowing words of his "white rising". He, then, went back to Tehran without winning any measure of religious or popular support. Two days after the Shah's visit to Qom, i.e. 6 Bahman 1341 HS (26 January 1963 C.E), his government held the referendum under heavy presence of its security apparatus and police forces, in spite of the total boycott declared by the religious scholars and political groups, a boycott which had won the solidarity of the masses. After that, Imam Khomeini met with the high ranking religious scholars of Qom and issued an important statement. They affirmed their refusal of the referendum process, explaining, in detail, i.e. in legal and religious terms, their position and the drawbacks of what the Shah dubbed a white revolution, in that it violated the articles of the constitution, ignored the interests of the nation and paid a lip service to the tenets of the Islamic *shari'a* law. This declaration was signed by nine high-ranking religious scholars of Iran, hence the name of "the declaration of nine signatories". Those who signed the declaration were:

1- Rohullah al-Mosawi al-Khomeini
2- Mohammed Redha al-Mosawi al-Gulpaygani
3- Mohammed Kadhim Shariatmadari
4- Mohammed al-Mosawi al-Yazdi (known as ad-Damaad)
5- Murtadha al-Husayni al-Langroudi

6- Ahmed al-Hussaini az-Zanjani
7- Mohammed Hussain At-Tabataba'i
8- Hashim al-Aamili
9- Murtadha al-Ha'iri.

Imam Khomeini continued to deliver his revolutionary speeches, seizing every opportunity to speak to the people, with a view to making them aware of the mischievous plans of the government, the evil intents the Shah had against the religion and its adherents and for the country and its people. With the days of the *Nawrooz* (Persian New Year's Day) celebrations nearing, Imam Khomeini had agreed with other religious scholars to declare the celebrations as a general mourning for the calamities that had befallen the Iranian people, the worst of which had been the flagrant violation of religious teachings, the annihilation of the believers and the imposition of the unbelievers' domination. He issued a revolutionary call in which he condemned the government, the Shah's mischievous intents in waging war against religion and religious scholars (*ulema*), sacrilege of sanctities, paving the way for foreign domination, having scant regard to the people's interests, and declaring the feast of *Nawrooz* as public mourning. This call reverberated widely amongst the Iranian people, especially the intellectuals.

On the twenty fifth of Shawwal [The month that follows the holy fasting month of Ramadan, in the Hijri Lunar Calendar], coinciding with 2 Farvardin 1342 Hijri Solar Calendar, and in a reaction by the regime, the henchmen of Shah broke into the main theology school in Qom, i.e. al-Faydhiyya School during a religious public celebration of the anniversary of the departure of Imam Ja'far as-Sadiq (*a.s.*). In that attack, a number of theology students and others were murdered; among those was Sayyid Younis ar-Rodbari; many other students and ordinary people were injured. On the same day, a similar attack by the henchmen   of the regime was launched on theology students of the at-Talibiyya School in Tabriz.

News of the attack on both the schools and the resulting deaths was fast spreading amongst the people. The events had contributed to heighten religious fervour against the government of the Shah and raise revolutionary morale to new plateaus.

Imam Khomeini made good use of this incident in his conversations with the people who were frequenting his house; he also utilised it in his statements to lay bare plans of the regime to eradicate Islam from its roots and impose imperialistic hegemony on Iran and its Muslim people. In his conversations, he was stressing the fact that it was necessary for the people to continue their revolutionary movement against the regime and its oppressive imperialistic policies.[1]

It is worthy to note here the solidarity of Shia religious scholars (*ulema*) in Iraq with the rising of the *ulema* in Iran, especially in Kerbala and Najaf, headed by Imam as-Sayyid Mohsin al-Hakim, who, after the massacre of the al-Faydhiyya school, sent Imam Khomeini and other religious scholars in Qom, a cable. In it, he condemned the Shah's policy, lent his support to the rising of religious scholars, and called on them to come on mass to Najaf. This he intended as a manifestation of their rejection of the Shah's policies against both the religion and the people, and a bid to prepare the ground for adopting a united stand in which all religious scholars should participate in

---

(1) Regarding Imam Khomeini's speeches and declarations on this occasion, and the popular and religious reactions in the aftermath of the attack on Al-Faydhiyya school, please refer to *"Barresi va Tahlili az Nehzat-e Imam Khomeini,* (Studies and Analysis of Imam Khomeini's Uprising) "*,* vol.1, p. 356-420.

confronting the Shah's repressive regime.

Imam Khomeini returned the compliments by sending a cable to Imam al-Hakim, thanking him for his support for the Islamic cause in Iran; however, he apologized for not immigrating to Iraq, stressing that the migration of the *ulema* of Qom to Najaf would spell great dangers and that it was neither in the interest of religion nor the people. He contended that the departure of the leading religious scholars from Iran would create a vacuum.

At the fortieth day anniversary of the martyrs of al-Faydhiyya school, Imam Khomeini issued an important statement in which he was determined to escalate the level of confrontation with the regime, by hinting that the Shah should bear the responsibility for the incidents. In the statement, he also made clear that he would continue the revolution. Religious scholars from various regions in Iran wrote letters to Imam Khomeini, expressing their support and solidarity for his cause. In reply, he wrote, " Israel's danger to both Islam and Iran is very close. A pact has been, or soon will be, formulated with Israel to confront the Islamic state. In keeping silent and reclusive, we shall lose everything. Islam has a right upon us, and the Prophet of Islam has a right upon us. These hard times during which we are witnessing the enormous efforts of the great Prophet being subjected to [the dangers of] annihilation, Islam's *ulema*, and all those who have affinity with Islam must shoulder their responsibility and carry out what is their due. I am determined not to be swayed from my position and not to be deterred from proceeding on my path until this brutal regime reversed its policies ".[1]

---

(1) *Sahif-e Noor* (The Book of Light), vol.1, p.44

The month of Muharram, 1382 HL (June 1963), was fast approaching. The regime had prepared for this important religious occasion by taking certain measures to control the situation and completely monitor public forums, Hussaini mourning gatherings, religious speakers and reciters of the tale of martyrdom of Imam Hussain (*a.s.*). On this occasion, Imam Khomeini issued a statement in which he condemned the regime's measures in restricting the Hussainite commemorative ceremonies. He called upon the preachers and reciters to remind the people of the dangers that were besetting Islam and Iran and what was befalling Islam and Muslims in those times. He stressed that Israel's danger to Islam and the Islamic *umma* (community) was no lesser a danger than that of the Umayyad rule which committed the crime of murdering Imam Hussain (*a.s.*) and his companions and was intent on uprooting Islam.[1]

In that year's month of Muharram, Iran had turned into an arena abounded with revolutionary fervour, translating into shouts condemning the regime which was considered as an embodiment of the Umayyad regime in its confrontation with the Messenger of Allah (*s.a.w.*) *and* his descendants. On the day of *Ashura* (the tenth of Muharram), revolutionary activity amongst the masses was rising high; they began demanding the downfall of the Shah and condemning his dictatorial practices, and declaring their allegiance to Imam Khomeini and their readiness for sacrifice and dying for the cause on the path to achieve the noble goals of his movement.

Imam Khomeini announced that he would address the masses at al-Faydhiyya school in Qom on the day of *Ashura*. The regime did its utmost to prevent him from this. But, he

---

(1) *"Barresi va Tahlili az Nehzat-e Imam Khomeini"*, (Studies and Analysis of Imam Khomeini's Uprising),vol. 1, p. 429.

refused, and was resolved on the necessity of addressing the masses on that day, irrespective of the consequences. Tens of thousands of people gathered inside and around the school to listen to his speech. In the afternoon of that day of Ashura 1383HL (1963CE), in the presence of a huge and highly charged gathering, Imam Khomeini delivered his historic speech in which he said, "This regime is an outright enemy of Islam, it is antagonistic to religious scholars (*ulema*). It wants to leave for Islam no trace; it wants to leave neither for the young nor for the old of this nation any trace. Israel does not want to leave for the Qur'an in the country any mention, Israel wants to leave for the *ulema* of Islam and its tenets no trace; it wants to leave for knowledge and religious scholars no trace in this country. Israel has wrecked al-Faydhiyya school through the action of its stooges. It is attacking us and our people. It wants to control your economy and destroy your trade and agriculture; it wants to plunder your wealth and remove all obstacles that stand in its way to achieve its goals. What prevents it from achieving its goals is the Qur'an; it, therefore, wants no existence of the Qur'an. What stands in its way and prevents it from achieving its goals are the religious scholars (*ulema*), the al-Faydhiyya school and other centres for religious learning; it is, therefore, adamant to remove these obstacles from its way in order to materialise its aims and make good its intents ...".[1]

Imam Khomeini continued his soul-stirring oration; the masses were transfixed to his words, shouting in approval at times, and weeping at others, until he finished his rousing speech, dotting the i's and crossing the t's so to speak, and attacking the Shah's regime with the use of eloquent rhetoric

(1) Ibid, p. 456

and wisdom. Cassette records of this speech spread far and wide around the country. It carried, with it to the hearts of people, a Hussainite zeal, religious sympathy, political enthusiasm and sincere determination unparalleled in the history of our Islamic *umma* in centuries past.

Through his orations and declarations, the Imam, had achieved many important aims; among these were the following:

1.   Breaking the barrier of fear in the hearts of the masses, and charging them with a high revolutionary zeal and moral drive.

2.   Destroying the false media aura concocted for the Shah. He did this through attacking him in person and holding him primarily responsible for all the cultural and economic backwardness that the people had been afflicted with throughout his rule. He also achieved it by holding the Shah accountable for all the crimes that had been and were still being committed by his regime's security apparatus.

3.   Revealing the regime's subordination to foreigners and imperialists, revealing its true face and false pretensions among the populace, thus destroying its popular base and influence amongst the masses.

4.   Forcing the regime, and its agents, to miss the chance to manipulate the people's passions and minds. He also sought to, and succeeded in, aborting the regime's plan for undermining the Islamic movement and its leadership, in that he made people aware of the regime's intent on planting the seeds of dissension amongst its various trends,

leadership and activist elements, and its use of disinformation and misinformation campaigns.

The Uprising of Fifteenth Khordad

The regime could not put up with Imam Khomeini's speech on the day of Ashura [the anniversary of the martyrdom of Imam Hussain] (of the year 1383 HL (1963-4 C.E.).). Only two nights after that speech, i.e. on the night of the twelfth of Muharram, coinciding with the fifteenth of Khordad (Persian *Hijri* Solar calender), the regime's henchmen broke into Imam Khomeini's house, at three o'clock in the morning, arrested him and headed towards the capital, Tehran. This was coupled with wide raids on houses of religious scholars, preachers and men of letters. On the same night, security elements arrested large numbers of religious scholars (*ulema*), Islamic movement activists of various backgrounds, especially religious scholars, orators and theology students. On the morning of the twelfth of the holy month of Muharram 1383 HL (5.6.1963), coinciding with (15 Khordad 1342 HS (1963 C.E.)), and no sooner had the news of Imam Khomeini's arrest spread, the masses in Tehran, Qom, Shiraz, Isfahan, Tabriz, Mashhad and other cities of Iran, rose up, thronging the streets, shouting long live to Imam Khomeini, death to the Shah, demanding the immediate release of the Imam, and condemning the Shah's dictatorship and repressive policies. On a different front, and by orders of the Shah, the regime decided to confront the popular uprising with fire arms, to break it up by all means and with unbridled violence and brutality, an action that led to the murder of many people, especially in Tehran and Qom. It went on record that the uprising of fifteenth Khordad was the first popular uprising that engulfed the country and was met with a bloody repression, since the Shah ascended to the throne in Iran.

Popular protests against the Shah government continued. They were expressing condemnation of the arrest of the Imam and demanding his release. Religious scholars (*ulema*) in Qom, Mashhad and other cities in Iran, as well as those of Najaf, Iraq, were voicing, in unison, their condemnation of the government and demanding the release of the Imam. The Shah government had intended to put an end to Imam Khomeini's life, had it not been for the steadfast stand of religious scholars and the masses against the Shah, especially the step taken by a group of religious scholars from Qom who marched on mass to Tehran to warn the government of the consequences, should it venture to harm the Imam, and demanded his quick release.

Consequently, on 18 Farvardin 1343 HS (7 April 1964 AD), the regime released Imam Khomeini. The regime had hoped that its brutal crackdown on the uprising of fifteenth Khordad, the arrests of hundreds of revolutionaries, and the exile of scores of them to outlying regions of the country, would put down forever the torch of popular revolution, and that Imam Khomeini's zeal in mobilising the masses in a revolutionary manner against the regime and its policies would falter. Yet, no sooner had the regime released Imam Khomeini, he returned to exercise his revolutionary activity, especially after the Iranian authorities had granted the Americans the right of immunity, or what was called "capitulation", which protected the Americans against prosecution before the Iranian judiciary, should they commit any violation in Iran. According to this "capitulation", the judiciary of Iran had no jurisdiction to put on trial any citizen of the United States of America, regardless of the type of crime he/she might have committed. Instead, the Iranian judiciary should refer the case to the American authorities to conclude whether or not the accused warranted a trial.

On 4 Aban 1343 HS (26 October 1964), Imam Khomeini delivered a political speech in which he condemned this imperialistic law and said, 'Our dignity has been dealt a blow, the Iran national pride has been trampled, the honour of the Iranian army has been violated. They, i.e. the regime, have ratified a law that makes us among the signatories of The Treaty of Vienna. It means that American military advisors, their families, staff and servants are immune and protected in Iran regardless of the crimes and violations they may have committed. I warn you of this danger. O Iranian soldiers! Be warned of this danger. O Iranian politicians! Be warned of this danger. By Allah, silence is a crime that is punishable by Allah. By Allah, he who does not shout his objection loudly is a sinner. O leaders of Islam! Save Islam. O religious scholars of Najaf! Save Islam. O religious scholars of Qom! Save Islam". [1]

On the same date, he issued an important declaration, in which he wrote, " Let the world know that our problems and miseries are all of the making of foreigners, the making of America. The Islamic *umma* (community) hates the imperialists in general, and America in particular. America is the one that supports Israel and its protectors. America is the one that supports Israel in evicting Muslim Arabs from Palestine. " [2]

Right after this revolutionary stand of Imam Khomeini, the Shah regime decided to exile him to Turkey on 4th November, 1964. In Turkey, he was put under house arrest, in the city of Bursa. He was kept under surveillance by members of the Turkish security forces until he immigrated to Iraq on 5th October 1965.

---

(1) *Kawthar*, vol. 1, p. 169.
(2) *Sahif-e Noor* (The Book of Light), vol. 1, p. 109.

On arrival in Iraq, Imam Khomeini settled in Holy Najaf, Iraq, the renowned centre for knowledge and learning, especially theology. There, dignitaries and religious scholars gathered together around him. He started giving lectures in jurisprudence. His Islamic Seminary (*hawza*) became one of the most important schools, and a league of its own.

In January 1969, he began formulating his study on *Walayatul Faqih* (The guardianship of the jurist). This has been based on his juridical theory regarding the rule in Islam on the principle of *al-walaya* (guardianship).

Imam Khomeini was not the first Imamite religious jurist to voice the principle of *Walayatul Faqih*. Many others had preceded him to this, most noted of these was al-Mawla Ahmed an-Naraqi, who had written an extensive study under this title, and the author of the renowned Encyclopaedia of Jurisprudence, *Jawahir al-Kelim*, or Pearls of Wisdom. But what distinguished Imam Khomeini from other religious jurists was his application of this theory and establishment of a modern state based upon the principle of *Walayatul Faqih*.

In addition to his academic work, he had continued in sending written and audio messages addressed to the Iranian people, urging them to continue the struggle against injustice in spite of the Shah regime's brutality in confronting Imam Khomeini's revolution, and all that is related to Imam Khomeini. Calls for the support of Imam Khomeini and his enlightened opinions had become a crime punishable by the Shah regime with the severest punishment. In this cause, many religious scholars (*ulema*), revolutionary intellectuals and young people, among the faithful, attained the status of martyrdom. In the forefront of those, who fell in this cause were Ayatollah as-

Sa'eedi and Ayatollah al-Ghaffari – two of the prominent religious scholars (*ulema*) of Tehran.

On the first of the month of Aaban 1356 HS (23 October 1977), Ayatollah Sayyid Mostafa al-Khomeini, eldest son of Imam Khomeini, suddenly and suspiciously died (suspicions were directed against the involvement of the elements of Savak [the Shah security arm]. He was one of the most resilient religious scholars (*mujahideen*), and a staunch supporter of his father throughout the revolution since its start. Soon after, the Iranian people began to show unprecedented sympathy towards his death. In all provinces and cities of the country, various sections of the people began to hold large scale commemorative and mourning ceremonies. These ceremonies were seized upon by the revolutionaries in spreading liberation opinions of Imam Khomeini, and in condemning the oppressive and imperialistic policies of the Shah regime. All over the country, a big torrent of empathy with the Imam and his ideas was embroiling, on the one hand, and torrents of general discontent and hatred towards the Shah, his regime and policies, on the other.

On this occasion, Imam Khomeini delivered an important speech to his students in Najaf, Iraq in which he considered the death of his son a Divine grace. He, also, outlined the objectives of his revolution, setting out to the Iranian people important recommendations. Outstanding among these was the necessity for revolutionary solidarity amongst all sections of the people in their struggle against the tyranny of the Shah and international hegemony. In those recommendations, he laid a particular stress on the imperativeness of solidarity between religious scholars and theology students on one the one hand, and intellectuals and university goers on the other.

The Shah regime found itself compelled to stand in the face of this outpouring of popular sympathy with the Imam and his revolution. It embarked on executing a media plan aimed at undermining the popularity of the Imam and the weight his influence had carried with the populace, a manifestation of which the strength of feeling shown at the death of Sayyid Mostafa al-Khomeini. An article, signed by a pseudonym, about the character of Imam Khomeini was published on 17 Daye 1356 HS (7 January, 1978) in *Ittila'at* Newspaper. In it, the writer wrote defamatory allegations about Imam Khomeini, which resulted in arousing the public opinion against the regime. The religious schools (*hawza*) in Qom suspended lectures in protest against the regime and for its being the instigator behind the publication of the article. On 19 Daye 1356 HS (9 January 1978), theology students and various sections of the people took to the streets of Qom. At the time, I was a witness, as well as a participant, with the masses, who were protesting against the regime and condemning its oppressive and tyrannical practices.

From there began the new uprising which the regime had faced with the most brutal of measures that included killings, imprisonment and torture. Popular protests and demonstrations were intensifying and spreading far and wide. Gradually, they encompassed all regions of the country. The month of Ramadan was near. Religious scholars, and speakers, made use of this occasion in deepening the revolutionary movement in the souls of the masses, fortifying the spirit of steadfastness, stressing the necessity to be patient and resilient, and calling on them to remain on the path until the attainment of the desired goals.

In his appeals, Imam Khomeini was stressing that the revolution is continuing until the downfall of the Shah and the establishment of an Islamic government that is just and operates in accordance with the Qur'an and Islamic dictates. He had clearly defined the objectives of the revolution in these two tasks, i.e. the downfall of the Shah government and the establishment a just Islamic government.

After the end of the month of Ramadan, the revolutionary elements seized the opportunity of the *Eid* prayers and transformed it into a resounding protest against the regime, expressed their determination to continue the popular protest by announcing the staging of a general protest march to take place on 17 Shahrivar 1357 HS (18 September 1978). The streets of Tehran were thronged with the demonstrators.

The Shah authorities confronted them with heavy tactics and violence, opening fire on them. As a result, tens, if not hundreds, fell dead. It became known as the massacre of the Month of Shahrivar.

The massacre of the month of Shahrivar had lent impetus to the revolution. Revolutionary zeal among various sections of the people became intense. Teachers, merchants, artisans and workers declared a general strike until the downfall of the Shah regime. Strikes spread wide to include staff and workers at the Iranian Oil Company. All this was in accordance with the Imam's directions, and via his continuous calls and messages to the people – whether written or tape-recorded – which were fast spreading in all parts of the country.

On the advice of the Shah government which had strong ties with the Ba'thist regime, the Iraqi government, started to bring pressure to bear on Imam Khomeini and demand him to refrain from his political activity against the Shah government. But, Imam Khomeini decisively refused to give in and insisted on continuing his political activity, declaring it was within his lawful right to do so; thus, he would not duck such a responsibility. At this point, the Iraqi authorities ordered Imam Khomeini to leave Iraq. He went to Kuwait, but the Kuwaiti authorities prevented him from entering its Territory. When Imam Khomeini had discovered that countries of the region refuse him entry because of his stand towards the Shah government, and because of their strong ties with the Shah and his government, he decided to go to Paris. On 13 Aaban 1357 HS (4 November 1978), he took a plane to Paris.

Imam Khomeini's revolution found resonance in some verses of the Holy Book, in that Allah's promises were evident, especially,

"And they planned a plan, and We planned a plan while they perceived not. See then how was the end of their plan that We destroyed them and their people, all of them". (27:50-51)

The more the tyrants (*mustakbireen*) plot, the more their plot rebound on them. They hatched a plan by limiting Imam Khomeini's scope for movement within the region. They miscalculated the move. Forcing the Imam to leave for Paris had presented him with a golden opportunity, in that he would make use of the international media, and communications means available there. On the one hand, he was able to put his case across to the world opinion, by explaining the goals of his revolution, denuding the practices of the Shah repressive authorities; he would, on the other hand, make use of the media forums available to him, the readily accessible communication facilities there to direct his address to the Iranian people with ease and at the opportune time. His exile to Paris was, at that period of time, an excellent opportunity for escalating the pace of the Islamic revolution and ensuring its continuity.

Since the revolution had entered its new phase on 19 Daye 1356 HS (9 January 1978), the countdown for government of the Shah began. This countdown had accelerated since the massacre of 17th Shahrivar. The Shah government lost its equilibrium by acting irresponsibly and aimlessly. The Shah started to dismiss one government after the other. During the year of the revolution he dismissed the Huvaida government, the Jamsheed Amozgar government, followed by the Sherif Imami government. All of that was to no avail; it neither helped putting down the flame of the revolution, nor did it help in regaining control over the country. The Shah resorted to the army, dismissed the Sherif Imami government, and replaced it with the government of General Azhari, who used excessive force in dealing with dissent, imposed martial laws on the country, prohibited gatherings, imposed night curfew, and deployed the army hardware in the major cities. Yet, all of this was of no use.

The people continued with their revolution under the leadership of Imam Khomeini, who was closely nurturing and monitoring it minute by minute, taking necessary action commensurate to circumstance and time and inching towards his aim. The Shah was forced to change course of his policy, in that instead of confronting the revolution head on, he decided to resort to more subtle ways, i.e. through deceit and trickery. He expressed his apology to the people, maintaining that he was aware of the problems that the people suffer from, promising to release political prisoners and follow a course of free and open political life, and inspiring hope to pave the way for freedom of expression. To pull the wool over the eyes of the people, he dismissed the army general, who headed the government, and chose for a prime minister a political figure that was ostensibly one of the opposition figures, namely Shahpur Bakhtiar. He thought that the people would be fooled by this deception, and that the leadership of the revolution would lose the moral argument through which it could arouse the populace and call on them to continue the revolution and stand firm on its path.

The ongoing strike and demonstrations began to have their toll in terms of loss of life and on the national economy. The people began to face real hardships because of the general strike that had spread to markets, institutes of learning, factories, plants, especially in the oil industry when the economic machine grounded to a halt; shortage of fuel in a bitter winter was one adverse aspect of the general strike.

On 26 Daye 1357HS (16 January 1979), the Shah of Iran fled the country. The people celebrated his departure and were immensely happy. The streets were crowded with people who were shouting "death to the Shah and long life and victory for Imam Khomeini".

In tandem with the Shah's departure, Imam Khomeini announced the formation of a revolutionary command council and made it clear that he intended to return to the country. The people welcomed this announcement, and began preparations for the reception party of the Imam. However, the Bakhtiar government announced its opposition to his decision, ordered the closure of airports and cancelled internal and external flights.

When informed of the Imam's decision to return to the country, the people began to fill the streets of Tehran, demanding the return of the Imam. Religious scholars and students of Qom marched on mass to Tehran and declared a continuous sit-in inside Tehran University, demanding the return of the Imam. They soon were joined by the university professors and students. Tehran was turned into a melting pot for revolutionary fervour that was bringing pressure to bear on the government to remove the obstacles and open up the way for the return of the Imam. The pressure paid off, in that the government was forced to climb down and allow the Imam to return.

On 12 Bahman 1357 HS (1st February 1979), the aeroplane that was carrying the Imam landed in Mihrabad airport in the capital Tehran. It was a day of feast (*Eid*) for the masses. Millions from all over the country had come for the reception of their victorious leader Imam Khomeini. He was received by the millions in an unprecedented manner. The masses lined up the road connecting the airport and the cemetery of martyrs to greet their victorious leader and pay him homage. From the airport, the Imam went straight to the martyrs' cemetery to deliver his first public speech after his arrival in the country and to outline the forthcoming steps for the revolution.

The masses gathered together there to listen to the Imam delivering a revolutionary political speech. In it, he stressed the need for changing the system of government and establishing instead an Islamic state, by people's consent. Four days later, i.e. 16 Bahman 1357 HS (5 February 1979), he announced the establishment of the Islamic state, and chose Sayyid Mahdi Bazirgan to be its first prime minister. No sooner had the Imam announced this move, the masses took to the streets, declaring their support and acclaim for this state.

On 19 Bahman 1357 HS (8 February 1979), large sections of the air force came out in support of the revolution and declared allegiance to Imam Khomeini. This had a great effect on the morale of the army. Hard on the heel, sections of the Iranian armed forces had begun to declare their allegiance to the Imam. The Imam issued an important declaration, calling on the soldiers to desert their military barracks and join the masses; he also appealed to military officers and commanders to do likewise and requested the people to behave responsibly and amicably towards the army as a whole, and consider the soldiers as brothers of the people and participating partners in the revolution. This had a great impact on winning large sections of the army over to the side of the people and in neutralising other sections of the army. Army commanders, who were still faithful to the Shah, felt helpless and that the prevailing spirit within the army rank and file was that of allegiance to the revolution and its leader, and to the people and their cause, on the one hand, and rebellion against the Shah and the commanders that were still faithful to his authority and government, on the other.

Victory of the Islamic Revolution

On the day of 21 Bahman 1357 HS (10 February 1979), the Army command declared strict martial laws, and imposed a general curfew in Tehran. But, Imam Khomeini called upon the people to defy the order totally, and take to the streets to protest against the regime and its unjust decisions. The masses responded favourably to the Imam's appeal and went out to the streets, condemning the unjust tyrannical regime. Sections of the Iranian army went to join the ranks of the masses. The morale of the masses grew even higher. They stormed military barracks and the state's military and security establishments. Police and army stations began to fall one after the other in the hands of the masses; the onslaught culminated in the revolutionaries' storming the building of radio and television in the evening of that day, the 21 Bahman.

News of the victory of the Islamic revolution, led by Imam Khomeini, was announced from radio and television. By a decree of the Revolution's Council, committees of the revolution were formed and assumed the running of the country, until the Islamic government, headed by Sayyid Bazirgan, started its functions and exercised its role of running the country's affairs.

From the very moment of the Islamic revolution's victory, Imam Khomeini began establishing the institutions of the Islamic state and laying down the foundations of the Islamic system. First, he announced the holding of a referendum to choose the type of system, i.e. whether Islamic or otherwise. The referendum was held on 12 Farvardin 1358 HS (1 April 1979), on choosing the Islamic Republic by (yes) or (no). There was a near unanimity on going for the system of Islamic Republic, i.e. 98.2% of the votes. The referendum was free and the first of its kind in Iran's history.

On a different front, parties hostile to Islam, such as nationalists, liberals and communists began hatching plots and intrigues, of all sorts, against the new Islamic system. Most troubling of these was the unrest in Azerbaijan, Kurdistan, Turkmen Sahra and Khuzistan, which these orchestrated under the pretext of demanding self-rule for Turkish, Kurdish and Arab nationalities. This was followed by certain sections of the Iranian army, loyal to the Shah, attempting a coup d'etat. But Imam Khomeini's wisdom, leadership and unwavering stand, augmented by loyalty of the masses to the revolution and its goals, foiled all these plots. The Islamic Republic was forging ahead to achieve its objectives.

The Islamic system's institutions were beginning to be formed one after the other. The people elected their representatives to the Council of Experts that was to decide upon the political system and draft an Islamic constitution. This was put to a referendum, in which the masses endorsed the Islamic constitution with an almost near consensus. In the light of the constitution, members of the Islamic *Shura* Council [parliament] and the president of the republic were elected. As such, the fledgeling institutions of the Islamic state began materialising. Thus, a modern Islamic state came into being. This state was the first of its kind in the modern era, rather the first in Islamic history after the era of the guided Imamate.

Abulhasan Bani Sadr was the first president of the republic of Iran. During his term, Saddam Hussain, the Ba'thist Iraqi President, waged a wide war on the Islamic Republic, with the intention of nipping it in the bud. He thought that the collapse of the Iranian army in the runup to, and in the aftermath of, the Islamic Revolution, coupled with the absence of any other military force to protect the country against foreign aggression, would present him with a golden opportunity in achieving a quick victory over the Islamic republic and occupy, with his Western and Eastern masters, the position of the victorious hero. What had encouraged him further was the presence of Bani Sadr at the helm of the country. Bani Sadr was not a believer in the revolution and its goals; he aimed at imposing his own brand of liberalism in running the country; he even was harbouring a desire to get rid of the Imam and revolutionary institutions and turn into an autocrat.

The Iraqi regime's forces continued to occupy large swathes of Iranian territory, including eleven cities, such as Khoram Shahr, Bustan, Sosangerd, Mehran, Dehluran, Islamabad and Qasr-e Shirin. The Islamic Republic was coming under attack on two fronts, an external enemy whose forces were still advancing inside Iranian territory, and a president, i.e. Bani Sadr, who was intent on attacking and eventually destroying the revolutionary institutions with the purpose of installing a secular government from a coalition of communist and national liberal parties. All efforts of Imam Khomeini, and other leaders of the revolution, did not succeed in bringing Bani Sadr to his senses, by persuading him to work within the remit of the Islamic constitution and law. Imam Khomeini was forced to relieve Bani Sadr of his post as the commander-in-chief of the army. Until then, he was acting on the Imam's behalf in the army command. This meant a vote of no confidence in him, a move that precipitated the convening of the Islamic *Shura* (Consultative) Council [parliament] to vote whether or not to grant him confidence.

On 20 Khordad 1360 HS (10 June 1981), the *Shura* Council voted to withdraw confidence from Bani Sadr. Thus, the government of Bani Sadr, first president of the Islamic Republic of Iran, collapsed.

Bani Sadr was in alliance with an organisation called *Mujahidi Khalq* that although, in essence, it upholds Marxist ideology, yet this is papered over by interpretations of Qur'anic verses. This organisation was aspiring to take power in Iran; it was receiving political and financial support from the West, amongst which was America. After the fall of the Bani Sadr government, *Mujahidi Khalq* declared war against the Islamic Republic; they put this to the test by assassinating revolutionary figures and religious scholars. On top of the hit list was Ayatollah Sayyid Ali Khamenei, who was then a prominent member of the Islamic *Shura* Council, Imam of Friday prayer in Tehran and representative of Imam Khomeini in the Supreme Defence Council and in the Army. The attempt resulted in some injuries that were soon treated, and left some effects on his right hand, leaving him maimed.

This was followed by the bombing of the headquarters of the Islamic Republican Party. That attack claimed the lives of seventy-two of the revolution's leading figures; among the dead was Ayatollah Dr. Beheshti, who was the strong right hand of Imam Khomeini and played a prominent role, beside the Imam, in leading the revolution.

After that, came the bombing of the Republic Presidential Building that resulted in murdering the president of the republic Sayyid Mohammed Ali Raja'i, the prime minister Sheikh Mohammed Jawad Bahunar. Scores of other atrocities were committed, resulting in tens of casualties among members of the leadership of the revolution and its supporters, such as businessmen and ordinary people.

In spite of all this, the revolution and the Islamic state persevered, advancing towards its goals with firm steps and eventually prevailed over political plotting and internal violence. Political conditions inside the country became totally stable shortly after the downfall of Bani Sadr and his fleeing the country. The leadership of the revolution managed to rebuild the Iranian army, improve the preparedness of the Revolutionary Guards and turn it into a striking military force that has been capable of protecting the country's internal security, guarding its frontiers from outside aggression, and fighting alongside the Iranian Islamic army as a firm and daring military force.

Only then the Iranian Islamic forces began scoring victories over the forces of the Iraqi regime, culminating in the liberation of all Iranian territory and taking the initiative of conducting the war where and when the Iranian forces saw fit, moving at times the military confrontation inside Iraqi territory.

On 20 July, 1988, Imam Khomeini announced a cease fire, after the Islamic Iranian forces had taught the Saddam regime and his forces unforgettable lessons.

On 31 December, 1988, Imam Khomeini sent a historical message to the leader of the Soviet Union, Gorbachev, in which he predicted the end of Communism. He called upon him to contemplate the religious realities, stressing that the problems besetting modern man, including the citizens of the then Soviet Union, emanate from unbelief in Allah. He warned Gorbachev against falling into the trap of American hegemony. In that message, the Imam said, 'In essence, your problem is not a case of ownership, the economy or freedom. It is, rather, the absence of true belief in Allah, the Exalted; it is the problem that has begun to drag Western society to the brink of the abyss and which would inevitably lead it to a blind alley."[1]

On 28 March 1989, Imam Khomeini announced that Sheikh Muntazari was unfit to succeed him in the leadership of the Islamic revolution and its state. Sheikh Muntazari resigned his position as heir apparent to which he was elected, by the Council of Experts, in July 1983. In his letter to Muntazari, Imam Khomeini reiterated his opinion that from the start he did not think that Muntazari was up to the responsibility, that he did not want to intervene in the jurisdiction of the Council of Experts, and that he had tried painstakingly, by various methods, to draw Muntazari's attention to points of weakness in his political stands and opinions and draw his attention to the

---

(1) *Aawai Tawheed*, (The Voice of Monotheism), published by the Establishment for Systemisation and Propagation of Imam Khomeini's Works.

corrupt elements whom he took as aides. The Imam tried to expose the extent of danger that would threaten the future of the revolution and the state as a result of the evil intents of those closest to Muntazari. But the advice went unheeded.

Muntazari was not able to rid himself of the web of political ambition seekers around him. That group of people was planning to seize the resources of the country. It also sought to discredit the Islamic revolution and undermine its objectives. The Imam had no alternative but to announce his unequivocal position vis-a-vis the unfitness of Muntazari to carry the torch after his departure, in shouldering the gigantic task and responsibility of leading the revolution and the Islamic state.

Death of Imam Khomeini

Not long after, the health of Imam Khomeini continued to deteriorate unto death where his soul found solace with its Creator (May He be pleased with him). He passed away on the evening of 4 June, 1989. Thus, a chapter was closed. The great heart stopped, a heart that was burgeoning with concern for the welfare of the meek (*mustadh'afeen*). Gone is the man who fought for the underprivileged. Gone is he who worshipped his Lord and worked diligently in His cause. Gone is the man who hoisted high the banner of working in accordance with the dictates of Allah's religion. The founder, with help from God, of the Islamic state, had departed. It is with the grace of the Lord, the believers were made mightier and through him had made the tyrants, dictators and the conceited lowlier.

In addition to his classical scientific works, Imam Khomeini had left behind a vast heritage of sayings, sermons and letters that comprise his political, social and educational opinions. These are considered among the most elevated of intellectual works that the human mind could produce. The most outstanding and important amongst these is his political and religious legacy.

So, as news of Imam Khomeini's demise spread, the Council of Experts immediately held a meeting, and elected, almost unanimously, Ayatollah Imam Sayyid Ali Khamenei successor to the Imam, and leader of the Islamic Revolution and its State.

« Chapter Two »

Examining Imam Khomeini's Project for Change

The project for transformation adopted by Imam Khomeini encapsulates two basic principles and a number of case studies. As for the two basic principles, they are:

1. Raising the human individual in a proper manner, i.e. commensurate to what Allah has ordained. This can only be achieved by way of training the soul to be righteous, well brought up and purified, within the principles, fundamentals and teachings outlined in the Holy Qur'an and detailed through the tradition of the Infallibles (May Allah's peace be with them). Imam Khomeini says, "The starting point for any reform is man himself. If man fails to reform and conduct himself in a proper manner, he would not be able to be a good example for others and lead them in the right way...You have noticed that throughout the rule of yester sultans and sultans [rulers] of late whom many of you have caught up with, and some of you have partly caught up with, that those who had assumed the responsibility of running the affairs of Muslims have been lacking in Islamic bringing up, and little did they possess of reform. It is because of this noticeable drawback, they have dragged our country to the state you have seen it in and brought our people to a state that cannot be mended for many years to come. That is why we all should start with mending our own ways and not be contented with mending the outside; rather, we must start from the hearts and minds of ours. We should strive to make our morrows better than today. I hope that we all should undergo this self-searching exercise, i.e. internal jihad,

which is to be followed by the jihad (struggle) for building the country." [1]

Sayyid Imam Khomeini (May Allah have mercy on his soul) had left behind a huge educational heritage that is unique among that of our scholars and educationalists, not to mention others.

The Forty *Hadeeth* (Tradition of the Prophet), The Secret of Prayer, Interpretation of the *Sahar* (dawn) *Du'a* (supplication) and the Greatest Jihad, are but some of his moralistic and educational works that cater for cultivating the soul, its spiritual preparedness in order to make it attain higher levels of purification and perfection.

He was heavily engaged in worship; his nightly devotion was a regular occurrence; he was renowned for his continual recitation of supplications and remembrance bequeathed by the Prophet (*s.a.w.*) and his Pure Progeny (*a.s.*). He was paying special attention to the holding of whispered prayer (meditation) that usually takes place during the month of Sha'ban whose merits and reward the Imams (*a.s.*) spoke favourably of. He was often reciting this supplication, "My Lord! Grant me utmost devotion to Thee. Fill our hearts with the light with which we look up to You, so that our insights could penetrate that which veils the light and reach up to the metal of the greatness, and our souls yearn to the glory of Your sanctity".

---

(1) Imam Khomeini's speech delivered at the meeting with the President of the Republic and members of the government on 23.10.1360 HS. Please refer to *Sahif-e Noor* (The Book of Light), vol.1, p. 282.

2. Building a virtuous society, by way of establishing a virtuous
    government that is based upon justice and the principles of
    Islam and the Holy Qur'an. There is no other path for
    building a virtuous society but through toppling the tyrant
    government and establishing a just Islamic government.
    Imam Khomeini said, "Both the Islamic dictates and reason
    make it incumbent on us not to let non-Islamic governments
    continue on the path that they are following, because a non-
    Islamic political system simply means the inevitability of
    banishing the Islamic political system. Furthermore, since
    every non-Islamic political system is a polytheist system by
    virtue of its subordination to a despotic government, and we
    are ordained to clear the traces of polytheism from the
    Islamic society; we are further ordained to prepare the
    virtuous social ground and sound educational environment
    for nurturing virtuous and believing people. Such a ground
    and environment are impossible to provide for under the
    shadow of a despotic government. It is unavoidable,
    therefore, that we must bring down corrupt and corrupting
    ruling systems, and remove the treasonous, corrupt, unjust
    and despotic rulers. This is the duty of Muslims in all the
    countries of Islam". [1]

He also says, "The tradition of Allah's Messenger (*s.a.w.*) is
unequivocal in stressing the establishment of the
government, for, historically, he was the first one to establish
such a government and undertake its administration... It is
also because he named the ruler after him". [2]

As for his field projects, they are many, and can be divided
into projects that ran throughout the different stages of

---

(1) The Islamic Government, pp.40-41, Beirut, 1971.
(2) Ibid, p. 28.

revolution and projects that ran throughout the stages of building the state. The revolution stage projects could be summarised as follows:

1. Using the organisation of Religious Authority (*marji'yya*) as a springboard for political mobilisation.

2. Relying on the masses and popular bases for principal support in the revivalist activism.

3. Arousing into action religious and popular organisations and employing them as a striking force and an effective arm in the field of revolutionary political action.

4. Establishing an effective ideological and social base which espouses the spreading of political and ideological opinions and aspirations of the Religious Authority.

5. Activating the network of religious scholars (*ulema*), throughout the country, with a view to utilising it as a link between the leadership of *marji'yya* and popular bases.

6. Politicising university students, with a view to thrusting them into the process of revolutionary change alongside theology students (*hawza*) and the network of religious establishment.

7. Avoiding confrontation with the armed forces, and attempting to neutralise the army as a first stage, then influencing it with the objective of winning it to the

side of the revolution, and taking it as a base among other revolutionary bases.

8. Initiating women into the realm of activity to play, in their own right, leading roles in participating in and transforming revolutionary work.

9. Espousing the project of Islamic state and *walayatul-faqih* as a well-defined framework for revolutionary political action and presenting a crystal clear idea of the nature of the much sought after political system.

As for projects to be put to the test during the phase of state-building, they are many and cover all kinds of institutions of the Islamic state. However, what we intend to set out here is to give an indication of the broad lines within which the establishment of the Islamic state had proceeded. In a summation, they are:

1. Setting-up institutions that bear the hallmark of the revolution, what it stands for, and that espouses its objectives, whether on the level of ensuring internal and external security, building and construction, or on the level of administration, the judiciary and codification.

2. Activating the striking forces and cadres in the revolution stage, to carry out the tasks of defending the state, protecting it and working towards the achievement of its aims during the stage of the state.

3. Using the institutions of the defunct government, after cleansing them of counter revolutionary elements, or those having a grudge against Islam. Reforming these

institutions should be pursuant to the aims of the Islamic state.

4. Devising the constitutional system in accordance with Islamic *shari'a* law and in a manner that ensures application of the *shari'a* in all aspects of life.

5. Establishing an Islamic civic society, and creating its institutions that are in harmony with the Islamic constitution, and the objectives and values of the Islamic revolution.

« Chapter Three »

Accomplishments of Imam Khomeini

Major Accomplishments

Indeed, the greatness of the man and the magnitude of his accomplishments pose, on the one hand, a difficulty for any person, who embarks on studying his life, to encompass them. On the other hand, if one decides to be selective, they might not have an easy ride too, for all his accomplishments were gigantic, in that it is rather hard to overlook or skim over hurriedly. That said, the major exploits of Imam Khomeini could be outlined as follows:

1. Arousing the Islamic *umma* (community) anew, and reviving the spirit of mobility, life and hope in it. Since the fall of the Ottoman Empire, especially after the usurpation of the land of Palestine, and the setbacks it had encountered in the military, cultural and economic confrontations with the enemy, the Islamic *umma* was reduced to a state of despair, disappointment, weakness, humiliation and subordination, that is rare to find the like of in other nations of all times and ages. Imam Khomeini's revolution was like a breath of life in the body of the *umma*, so much so that it has brought it back from the brink of death and restored its Islamic identity, sense of pride and might, and finally confidence in itself, its religion, prestige and dignity.

2. Bringing up and grooming a steadfast and believing members of a popular base, who manifest Islam as a faith

and conduct, and who work in the cause of Allah, unhindered by any criticism or reproach. This wide popular base, whose members were groomed by the Imam, was the one that stood fast in the face of all the tribulations and adversities that the revolution the Islamic state, and its institutions and interests, had to endure and eventually weather. Had it not been for this faithful and steadfast elite base, those tribulations would have exterminated the revolution and its aims. This steadfast popular base continues to provide an ongoing insurance policy that maintains the continuation of the revolution and the steadfastness of the state.

3. Putting an end to the myth of separating religion from state or politics, and setting an Islamic practical and theoretical base for this inseparability. Indeed, on a human level, reason dictates that establishing social justice, shorn of religion and Providence, is impossible.

4. Reviving the notion of Islamic unity, by practically implementation on the ground, both politically and socially, and internally and externally. This has been achieved through setting-up the required institutions and following up policies that cater for the unity of the *umma* (community).

5. Bringing down the age-old royal ruling system in Iran in spite of the unlimited support it was receiving from the majority of the great powers. Of significant importance to note here is that, in executing his revolution, Imam Khomeini did not rely on a specific political organisation, nor did he depend on any military or economic power, whether internally or externally. He used but the faithful word and revolutionary awareness that emanate from total devotion to Allah, the Most High, and recognition of a religious, as well as personal duty.

6. Establishing the Islamic system on a constitution based
    on the Holy Qur'an and the tradition of the Prophet (*s.a.w.*).
    Bringing into being an Islamic state and founding a new
    Islamic civil society that is ruled by Islamic system in all its
    spheres.

Assessing Imam Khomeini's Enlightened Opinions and Accomplishments.

No doubt that the enlightened opinions Imam Khomeini
came up with and the accomplishments he had rendered to
humanity and Muslims deserve much review and study, firstly,
to draw inspiration and learn lessons from, and, secondly, to
put right possible errors and develop the tasks for future stages.

Doubtless, again, what distinguishes most of the opinions
and accomplishments of the Imam is the fact that they have
proved their credibility and practicality in the real world. We
have not heard of any project that was worth earning but a
minute measure of success in comparison with that attained by
the opinions and practical projects of the Imam.

This characteristic leaves no room for the researcher but to
submit in high regard to this man's greatness and have respect
for his genius and various aspects of his unique personality.
Perhaps future times may give an opportunity for a realistic
critical assessment by researchers who are better equipped than
the ones of today when they might see that the experience of
the Islamic revolution and its state was the best witnessed by
contemporary man on the level of revolution and state. That is,
notwithstanding the minor blemishes that had tarnished the
image of this revolution and this state, that might have been

difficult to, or could not be, overcome in any other human experience that is subject to the measures of the possibly attainable, and not benefit from infallible guidance bestowed by Divine revelation.

To Allah, the Exalted, do we pray that He may grace us in the near future to review this blessed experiment through a critical assessment consistent with the size of the experiment and the greatness of the accomplishment.